INTENTIONALLY MINDING THE BUSINESS OF ME

10 strategies to help build a mindset that leads to the most favorite version of you

Samiyrah Bennett, MSW, LCSW

Foreword by: Dr. Terry Gadson, PhD, CASAC, LMHC

ISBN: 979-8-9856617-0-5

Editor Credit: Yakisha Bookard
Photography by: Jihaad Muhammad
Cover Design: Yaasmin Lewis

Distributed by The On Purpose Shop, LLC.

DEDICATION

This literature is dedicated to those who have doubted themselves for far too long and are now looking to commit to loving and caring for themselves more. If you're reading this right now, you're interested in learning the foundational tools to attain self-development while prioritizing mental health. The context of this book should be used to help you take care of the business of you. Learn how to utilize healthy coping skills and implementing strategies to preserve yourself while getting out of your own way to break cycles that have been keeping you in toxic patterns. If you're committed to do the work, I'm committed to help you navigate to the most favorite version of you. The version that truly makes you proud.

Table of Contents

ACKNOWLEDGMENTS

My Bubbs - My 6-year-old daughter. Both courageous and confident, she shows up just as she is unapologetically. I love that about her! Every day, she gives me insight into the person I am becoming. This has drawn me closer to my most favorite self. She is my reason for so many things.

I must acknowledge Spirit. Because the way that Spirit has been working through me is how this project was able to be manifested. My therapist has provided a mirror for me to enhance my overall wellness and be honest with myself. My accountability partner, Rashida Henry, LPC - Thank you. My sister, Yaasmin - You get it and continuously empower me. I appreciate you.

TRIBUTE

My mother. You committed to motherhood and have provided your children with all the tools you had. The way you intentionally raised Queens who know their worth is what has gotten me to where I am today. Being a mother has shown me that it was not the easiest journey for you, but you did it the best way you knew how. Your hard work has not gone unappreciated. You've created me to carry the torch and provide even better for the next generation. I'm honored to be your daughter and to continue creating legacy.

NOTES TO THE READER

This book was written from a place of enlightenment after experiencing darkness. I've been at the place where I was "sick and tired of being sick and tired." Then, it came a time that I was ready to do something about it. After countless conversations with others, it became apparent that I was not alone in the way I was feeling. So, I created a wellness blueprint and promises to myself of how I wanted to live which I declared "Minding the Business of Me." It was made clear that this blueprint of the foundational steps to navigate towards my most favorite version of self was not just for me. It was to be shared with you.

What has happened to you may have been out of your control. However, choosing to heal from your experience(s) is in your control and is your responsibility. Take charge of your life and explore the foundational steps to connecting with you.

I know you've been asking yourself how or where to start. The following literature will provide the steps you need to move further along in your journey. You are so much more than what you have been through and are deserving of creating a life that you love. I hope you know that and decide to give yourself permission to start *now*. Right at this moment. Choose your wellness and take good care of yourself.

Two notions you'll have to get rid of to receive the messages and knowledge in this book – close-minded beliefs and your comfort zone. You will need to be open to doing something different than what you've always done. Remember, if nothing changes, then nothing changes.

Problem It Solves: This book helps you realize that you do not have to suffer in silence. It provides opportunities for you to gain resources to live life on purpose. It is through intentional living that you can connect

1

with the version of yourself that you love most. My hope is that you use this book as a blueprint to live well.

How To Use It: Read each chapter and recite the corresponding affirmations provided at the end. Also included are lined sheets that you can use to add your own affirmation, thoughts, and/or reflections that arise while reading. Hold yourself accountable and follow up with the notes you write down.

PERMISSION SLIP

I give myself permission to be open-minded while reading the contents of this book. I am committed to providing space for myself that allows me to recognize my value and worth. Throughout this journey, I give myself permission to release old narratives and make room for new energy that leads to my thriving season. I give myself permission to explore ways to support myself and change the narrative that helps me connect to my most favorite self.

Signed with Love and Commitment,

_____

[Sign your signature above]

PRE-ASSESSMENT

This assessment is to take inventory of how you are currently feeling about your personal journey.

Instructions - Circle "Y" for **Yes** and "N" for **No** for each question asked.

Have you been feeling like you desire more in life but unsure how to attain development in your personal life?

Y   N

Are you interested in prioritizing your mental health?

Y   N

Have you been yearning to connect with people and experiences that bring you joy?

Y   N

Have you been feeling "stuck" and not quite sure what the alternatives are?

Y   N

Interested in connecting with your authentic self unapologetically?

Y   N

Are you feeling like you're always "in your head" and looking to just live the life you desire by successfully managing the "noise"?

Y   N

If you answered "Y" to 3 or more of these questions, you would benefit greatly from this book. It is divinely connected to you. Keep reading to digest gems that will lead to your personal development, spiritual connection, and transformative wellness.

PREFACE

I must share this. It's by no coincidence that this book is entitled *Intentionally Minding the Business of Me.* For so long, I have minded the business of others. What do I mean by that? For a very long time, I have found myself always wanting to help others. Yes, helping others is highly desired; however, it becomes a problem when you begin compromising yourself and your needs over everyone else.

From a very young age, I knew I was called to be a helper. Life experiences, therapy, prayer, and self-reflection has taught me that I cannot continue giving to others without giving to myself first. For me, this equated to the importance of *minding my business* through tending to all my systems that include mental, emotional, physical, and spiritual. My well-being is THE business that I must attend to, and it MUST come FIRST!

FOREWORD

*Taking care of Yourself should not be considered a luxury. It's
your divine right and you owe it to yourself.*

What do you mean taking care of yourself is not a luxury? Of course, it is
a luxury! Well, at least it is for me because I have so many other things
besides myself to attend to. I have kids; I have a family; I have friends;
hell, I even have co-workers, a pet, and the list goes on and on. Oh, wait,
and the best one of all is: "It's selfish to put myself first. I'm ok. I'll just
do without." These are just some of the stories we tell ourselves to justify
neglecting our desires, needs, and wants.

Self-care can be defined as providing adequate attention to one's own
physical and psychological wellness (Beauchamp & Childress, 2001). It's
amazing how many people equate self-care and self-love with "sel-fish"
when that is the furthest thing from the truth. How can you save a
drowning person when you don't even know how to swim? How can you
save someone who doesn't want to save themselves? Why would you put
yourself in harm's way to hold onto someone or something that is
running from you just as you are trying to run to them?

I don't know about you, but I can relate to most if not all of the questions
above. There was a time when I was so caught up in other people's
problems that I had no idea how out of control my life had become. I
was living with 3 roommates who were a little younger than me and I
decided to put myself in charge of making them live their best lives even
though mine was a wreck. I referred to them as my "adult kids." Who
does that? Me, that's who. I mean living someone else's life is so much
easier than living your own. Right? Wrong! My life did not come full
circle until I started intentionally minding the business of me.
As someone who has known the author for the past ten years, I have
been a witness to her transformation from the inside out. She went from

becoming a social worker, to becoming a mother, to creating, developing, and running a successful private practice and now she can add phenomenal author to her list of accomplishments. I am a licensed mental health counselor and I always tell my patients "Your thoughts become things." *Intentionally Minding the Business of Me* offers the perfect blueprint on how to move out of your own way by transforming self-defeating thoughts and start living your life on purpose.

> *"Do not go where the path may lead, go instead where there is no path and leave a trail."*
>
> *Ralph Waldo Emerson*

Peace and Blessings,
Dr. Terry Gadson, Ph.D., CASAC, LMHC

INTRODUCTION

Your most favorite self is meeting your most honest needs and you unapologetically moving towards what that means for you. It is leaning into the uncomfortable parts of you and peeling back the layers with grace and compassion. As you move towards the most favorite version of you, understand that the definition of this can change depending on what you need in the associated season of your life. This may require you tapping into who you truly are which could mean uncovering some things that you've been hiding behind. The journey of connecting with your most favorite self is filled with looking deep within and showing up on purpose so you can be authentic to who you are. It includes confidence, knowing your worth and understanding that you are the only one that's in control of putting the limits on your life. It's understanding that when you truly choose to live intentionally that you can attain all that you desire. Your most favorite self requires you to do the work that allows you to meet all of your needs and all the ways that your needs require meeting.

Use the below space to define what it means to be your most favorite self. What do they look like? What do they believe about themselves? How do they walk into a room? Why are they the most favorite version of you?

_____

_____

_____

_____

_____

_____

_____

_____

_____

_____

_____

_____

_____

_____

_____

What does it mean to be 'intentional'?

To be intentional, simply means to live your life on purpose. So many people go through life aimlessly waiting for things to just happen. When you create a life of intention, you are consciously choosing how you want your life to unfold. And then taking the necessary steps to achieve it.

Chapter 1

"The notion you want to get really clear about is, you master what you practice. Practice speaking well to yourself."

- Samiyrah Bennett

Affirmations

In this book, you will notice that there are affirmations throughout. Let them serve as a reminder that you can create space where you intentionally speak to yourself. I am going to tell you like I tell myself and my clients, you must be extremely intentional about what you are telling yourself because your brain is always listening and recording. Our brains are designed in a way to automatically go to the negative and are instinctual in remembering the negative interaction in our life's experiences more than the positive ones. So, you see, it is vital for you to formulate an experience that includes paying special attention to what you are saying to yourself and how you are saying it. Engaging in the practice of reciting affirmations allows your brain to recognize the positive even during challenging times.

The Merriam-Webster Dictionary (n.d.) defines 'affirm' as, "to say that something is true in a confident way and to show a strong belief or dedication to an important idea." This is the exact concept when you decide to engage in affirmative exercises. There is so much power in deciding what you want to manifest (see happen) in your life and how you want to feel. Affirmations allow us to make room for these statements that will promote encouragement, improve motivation, establish positive self-talk, and amplify a sense of gratitude.

Some challenges that people face when starting to practice is that they do not instantaneously believe whatever affirmation(s) they are practicing. I want you to know that this is an appropriate response. It's almost like riding a bike. When you first learned how to ride a two-wheeler bicycle, you were unsure that you could do it. It didn't feel the same as when those training wheels were on. You wanted to master it but there was a feeling anchored in uncertainty that came to you. It wasn't until you believed that you could do it, with continuous practice, and deciding on mastering the skill of riding the two-wheeler, that you succeeded. It wasn't until the point you truly believed that you could that you were able to ride that two-wheeler freely and with confidence.

I remember when I first started engaging in daily practices of reciting affirmative phrases in my life. All kinds of self-defeating talk started to arise such as, "this is ridiculous," "you don't even believe what you are saying," and "I'm really in here talking to myself" - just to name a few. I'm sharing my experience with you because I want to normalize the idea that no matter who you are, your brain will sometimes tell you that you're doing something wrong, when it's the mere fact that you are doing something different than what your brain is used to. What's amazing is that you can retrain your brain. This is exactly what begins to happen when you commit to the practice. Self-affirming activities can feel different and that's because it's a new activity for you. Incorporating affirmations into your daily routine will help you to automatically challenge what comes up in a negative.

Personally, I went from feeling very uncomfortable reciting affirmations to incorporating it in daily practices all throughout the day. I literally have post-its and personalized notes hanging up all over in my home, car, phone, and office to hold myself accountable. I find it extremely helpful to remember to practice as well if I am always seeing reminders to affirm myself.

You're invited to find a practice that you're comfortable starting that involves affirming yourself. With continued practice, you'll begin to see your affirmed thoughts manifest in your life. It can also be very helpful to record yourself speaking well to yourself. Research shows that when people hear themselves repeating affirmations to affirm self, there is a direct correlation with boosting mood and increasing motivation (Cascio et al., 2016). It's not only about repeating them but believing in them.

Believing in yourself really. Again, get in the habit of treating yourself well. Affirmations promote psychological well-being. Self-affirmation theory in psychology proposes that if someone creates statements and values about themselves that they admire, they are less affected by someone who comes along with contradictory statements.

You may be asking yourself if you should 'fake it until you make it.' My response would be – No. Instead, practice until it becomes your reality. Intentionally choose how you want to show up in your experience. You're creating space to allow yourself to believe in you, your capabilities, and a higher power. This all taps into those systems we're going to discuss further in *Chapter 3: Mental* influences emotional which influences spiritual as well as physical. You'll have to be determined to show up on purpose in your experience.

When practicing affirmations, keep them specific, short, and focused on what you want to feel or experience. Also, they should be something realistic. Sometimes people tell me that they have tried affirmations and they just do not work. It may not be that they don't work; however, it may be that you're not engaging in the practice appropriately. Or it can also mean that you are not practicing long enough to give them an opportunity to work in your experience.

In 2009, The European Journal of Social Psychology published a study addressing forming new behaviors into automatic actions. The findings determined on average it takes 66 days to have a new behavior form into an automatic practice (Lally, Phillipps, et al., 2009). Other research suggests that it can take as little as 21 days to form a new habit or behavior.

My question to you is if you are willing to commit to 30 - 90 consecutive days of being intentional about what you're telling yourself to start seeing positive change in your journey of life? See, that's the thing. You must be willing, vulnerable, committed, and determined to the process of change for affirmations to work in your favor.

When it comes to beginning to practice affirmations, here are some helpful tips in your approach of reciting them. YES, there is a specific way to recite affirmations to yourself.

1. Develop awareness of what you want to specifically affirm.
2. Ensure the affirmative statement is in the present tense.
3. Affirm what you want and not what you don't want.
4. Commit to practicing daily so you can develop a routine.
5. Say them out loud.
6. Start off saying them in front of the mirror until you become comfortable.
7. Practice and then practice some more.

Some examples of affirmations may look like:

❖ I am giving myself permission to heal and rest without feelings of guilt.
❖ I am consistently becoming the person I love the most.
❖ I am committed to living my life intentionally.

Notice the "I am" before each phrase. These two words train your mind to accept whatever is coming after "I am" as the present moment making it more realistic and believable.

Repetition of affirmations and personal mantras to yourself can equip you with great healing powers. The implementation of scripting and reciting affirmations can activate processes in your brain and nervous system in efforts to shift mindset. The practice of reiterating an affirmational phrase can help connect with new thought patterns by developing new neural pathways in the brain. Neuroplasticity is the term used to describe forming new thoughts and ideas through practicing alternative ways of engaging in your environment. It is supported by research that the brain is able to be remodeled by changing internal and external factors (Kays et al., 2012). Rosa et al. (2013) refers to neuroplasticity as the dance between the brain and environment. It is referenced that the ability of the brain to be shaped by experience, and in turn, for this newly rewired brain to facilitate the embracing of new experiences. Overall, the brain is restructuring and forming new connections as a response to the new activity occurring in the environment such as reciting affirmations.

Your brain will be formulating new ways of thinking and behaving. The repetition will cause the pathway to get stronger until the new behavior being practiced is accepted by the brain as the new behavior.

The science behind affirmations truly supports the healing properties of the practice. What happens is, all the neural pathways that are sending signals in our brains are linked to thoughts and behaviors that we are used to. Every time you think something, feel something, or do something more and more, the pathway is strengthened. As you begin to shift behavior and form new habits, old pathways move to the side to make room for the new habits being practiced. When there is specific focus established to direct change, humans can most definitely rewire their brain to support their overall wellness and improve functioning.

As mentioned earlier, your brain is always recording and on 'go mode', so watching how you speak to yourself is vital in living well and taking good care of yourself. Providing intentional time to be present, engaging in practicing these mantras allows the ability to slow down. Reciting affirmations is a practice that is near and dear to me. I have seen the evidence of how helpful reciting exactly what you want to yourself unfolds. It really has become a form of praying meditation for me. It's encouraged that you use them in this way as well. The notion you want to get really clear about is, 'what you practice, you master.'

Affirmations reinforce what we want and how we want to show up in our lives and provide us with reassurance that what we want is feasible. You'll see affirmations throughout this entire book that correspond with the chapter content previously discussed. This is done on purpose to remind you that what you want is feasible and invite you to put reciting affirmations into practice.

In my private therapy practice, I help women get out of their own heads and into their lives. The strategies and treatment approach that I use help my clients to connect to their most favorite selves and live life on purpose. Within this work, combating negative self-talk and developing a relationship with self that holds space for love and kindness is vital. Therefore, it is one of the first topics of focus with therapy clients.

Creating an awareness about what you tell yourself during the human experience is an essential part of minding your business and living well. The more you repeat self-affirming statements, it allows your brain the opportunity to take these purposeful statements as facts.

Grace and removal of self-judgment is required when practicing affirmations. The reiteration of these statements will not only frame where you want to go, it will also allow you to claim it over your life.

Remember that dictionary definition we discussed in the beginning of the chapter? Let me remind you, 'to affirm' is to say something is true in a confident way. To show a strong belief or dedication to an important idea.

In all, you will need to become determined and committed to being connected to the change you want to see. Not just saying something and waiting for magic to start happening. It's saying something and then doing something about it. Practice means we are also incorporating changed behavior to match the affirmation being stated. Now that there's increased understanding of affirmations and how to apply them, let's get down to business.

Take this time to write down any reflections or notes about

Chapter 1: Affirmations.

Self-reflect on the Affirmations you want to create for yourself.

_____

_____

_____

_____

_____

_____

_____

_____

_____

_____

_____

_____

_____

_____

Chapter 2

"Minding your business is essential to living well, taking care of yourself, honoring your needs, and staying committed to the path that best serves you."

- Samiyrah Bennett

Minding the Business of You

"Your mind is a garden; Your thoughts are the seeds. The harvest will bring either flowers or weeds."

We're all going to die; so, what will you do while you're living?

I hope that caught your attention. I'll say it again: We are all going to die; so, what will you do while you are living? This is a very important question to ask yourself.

While life is short, the time we do have on the earth side allows opportunity for us to connect with the version of ourselves that we love the most. We are provided with opportunities to live life on purpose and be intentional with how we choose to show up in the world. Being intentional with how you live your life starts by minding the business of you.

The primary basis of taking good care of yourself is based on minding your business. What do I mean by that? There is absolutely no way that you can emotionally excel and personally develop if you are so focused on other things and people. Repeatedly engaging in the behavior of tending to other people's needs and things will keep you in a constant cycle of neglecting the business of you. I want to encourage you to understand that you are deserving of behavior that is much more supportive and compassionate rather than neglectful. Because of this it would be crucial for you to implement the tools and skills necessary to cultivate the experience of focusing on you and your needs.

To tend to your business, you will be required to take inventory of your needs. An understanding of who you are and deciding how you are willing to give yourself the things that are in your best interest is also a requirement in progressing on your journey. You'll have to tend to your own garden to heal from what you have been through and fall in love with who you are becoming. Are you ready to take the foundational steps needed to move forward in your healing journey? If you answered 'yes', you picked up the right book.

The business of you involves paying particular attention to your experiences, your thoughts, and your journey. With an understanding of where you are in your self-care journey and healing process, it is important for you to know that handling your business is essential. It is essential to living well, taking care of yourself, honoring your needs, and staying committed to the path that best serves you.

You are not what you have been through or what has happened to you. It's for that very reason that you are choosing to read this book. Whether you are committed to incorporating all things self-help into your life or simply curious from reading the title, you are in this moment for a reason.

I ask that as you continue to read through the context of the literature that you bring love and kindness with and to you. Can you also bring understanding that you are on a unique journey? This is your journey in your life, which means that no one else has to understand why you are moving the way that you choose to move. However, it is extremely important that you comprehend why you are on this journey and what you want out of this life you are living. Spoiler alert: You don't have to have it all figured out now. I invite you to make room for one step that may help you get your personal business in order. Along with all the feelings that come along with your circumstance, the path that you are on is yours. You get to narrate and parent yourself as you see fit for your needs. Your garden will not look like that of your neighbors. Reminding yourself of this will help you stay focused on the business that is you.

The methods used during my counseling services follow a framework named the "B.U.S.I.N.E.S.S." Framework. This framework can help you bring attention to your needs and what you may be required to modify in order to begin making the steps towards the version of you that will become your most favorite.

The framework uses the word 'business' as an acronym. The person you ideally would like to become will command you to **B**e Aware of Your Needs, **U**nderstand Curiosity and Reflection, **S**eek Solutions to Your Challenges, **I**gnore What Doesn't Align, **N**otice How You Respond to Different Situations and Experiences, **E**xtinguish Toxic Patterns, **S**et Boundaries and **S**ucceed in Being You. Gaining understanding of the 'Business' framework is essential to develop the foundational mindset that leads you to your most favorite self.

Here's a breakdown:

B – Be Aware of Your Needs

❖ Nothing happens before awareness transpires. This is the notion for all things that you want to modify. In order to change your outcome and attain your true desires, it is mandatory that you have an awareness of the necessities required for improvement of your overall functioning. To be aware of self is to be curious of one's emotions, thoughts, and behaviors. Being aware of your needs requires honesty as you move to being a radical observer of your mind. If you looked at yourself through a mirror, what supportive feedback would you want to provide to your reflection?

U – Understand Curiosity and Reflection

❖ Approaching your circumstances with a lens of curiosity allows you to become the observer and not absorb all that you experience. Does that make sense? Choosing to intentionally notice what happens in your life, allows you the opportunity to appropriately respond vs. impulsively reacting. Engaging in the practice of curiosity will open opportunities for you to be reflective because you are consciously choosing a state of awareness to your experience. Self-reflection is one of the most powerful skills to master as you cater to the business of you. When we choose to explore the notion of self-reflection and curiosity, we schedule time to intentionally pause. Most of us are in constant movement with daily life, so you may miss the opportunity to develop meaning from your experiences, sort through interpretations of life's happenings, and acknowledge your observations. Curiosity and reflection let you no longer act with this form of disregard.

S - Seek Solutions to Your Problems

❖ Our minds are designed in a way to automatically focus on the negative. Your brain will habitually go to "what's not working" before it tries to solve a problem or overcome a challenge. Sometimes, this can lead to cognitive distortions, which is another way of saying 'faulty and negative thought patterns.' It takes tenacity, persistence, and dedication to solve the problem as well as a commitment to do the work required to achieve your outcome. What would happen if every time you were faced with a problem you turned it into a challenge? Asking yourself, what would it look like if this area was going well? What's the FIRST step I need to make? By answering those questions to yourself, you allow opportunity for problem solving and critical thinking skills to arise. In turn, this helps you deal with the situation at hand. Instead of automatically focusing on what isn't working, you open yourself up to seek alternatives. This is an absolute necessity in taking care of your business to show up for yourself. This practice also helps to retrain how your brain supports your overall wellness.

I - Ignore What Doesn't Align

❖ Alignment is a concept that leads you to find the flow in your life rather than forcing things to happen. Ignoring what doesn't align with the specific season of your life that you're experiencing will present the ability to focus on removing the expectations of others.

❖ Can I be honest with you? As you move through your healing process, it will be important to comprehend that those people, places, and things that are not aligned with the healing version of you will have to be removed. On the journey of tending to your business, it's going to be incredibly important to trust that you know what's good for you without the influence of others. Exploring the ways you can learn to trust yourself will command you to spend time with yourself, be realistic with your goals and focus on your strengths. When you do this, you are beginning to remove the roadblocks that are keeping you away from your true self. For example, there are people that you are currently allowing to stay in your life when you know that it is in your best interest to close that chapter. Keeping this type of company in your life only brings turmoil, confusion, and stress related emotional states.

❖ Choosing to continuously engage in behaviors that no longer serve your wellness stands in the way of what is aligned for you. I am here to remind you that you are deserving of not betraying yourself and your true needs. Saying 'yes' to something or someone when you really want to say 'no' is considered abandoning yourself. In efforts to not abandon self, ignore what doesn't align with who you truly are and different levels of where you want to go. You get to say 'no' to the things that don't fulfill you in your current experience so that you can say more yes to you. Ultimately, this is what supports your truest self and helps you avoid people, places, and things that are unhealthy for you.

N – Notice how you respond to different situations and experiences

❖ A major component of intentionally taking care of your business includes learning how to respond as opposed to react. Paying attention to how you respond to situations can help decrease stress, allow you to gain control and reduce conflict that may show up with the people in your lives.

❖ The major difference between responsive and reactive is, reactions typically occur automatically and without thought while response requires awareness and intentional thought. When there is a deliberate shift from being reactionary to responsive, you're able to move from subconscious impulsivity (reacting without much thought processing) to more conscious behavior (intentional and supportive actions). When functioning in the realm of subconscious impulsivity, you rob yourself from learning new and more effective ways of communicating. However, when you decide to engage in a more responsive manner, you are deciding to pause and take inventory of your experience and notice what is happening around you so that you can respond in the most supportive and loving way for you. A technique that I often use with my clients is called the S.T.O.P method. It's a mindfulness skill that serves as a reminder to notice your feelings before you respond. The method is an acronym that stands for:

Stopping: When you feel your body becoming overstimulated, irritated, or annoyed, stop yourself. You can say your name, squeeze your fingers together and/or make sure both feet are planted on the ground. Ground yourself and come back to the present moment.

Take A Breath: Pause and Breathe. Inhale through your nose to the count of 4. Hold your breath for 4 counts and then exhale through your mouth for 6 counts.

Observe: Instead of being absorbed by what's currently happening. Take a step back and notice what feelings you are having without any judgement or impulse to act. Simply notice the feeling you are experiencing.

Proceed: This is when you get to put self-compassion into practice. During this part of the process, you're going to move forward with the best action that will be supportive to your wellness and more responsive than reactive.

❖ As a reminder, when beginning a new practice, it will take some time before you master. Be patient with yourself. Allow yourself to be a student and to continue to practice. While we're practicing, let's use an affirmation in this moment: *I give myself permission to be a beginner and I realize that it is by practicing that I become the expert.*

E – Extinguish Toxic Patterns

❖ Patterns of toxicity are repeated behaviors that you engage in although you are aware they work against your best interest. These patterns are directly correlated to supporting an unhealthy emotional state. It will also damage your mental, physical, and spiritual health. Engaging in toxic patterns may be a part of who you've become at this moment; conversely, they do not have to be a part of who you are now becoming. The most favorite self that you are aiming to connect with will require you to rid yourself of old behaviors, techniques, mindsets, and patterns.

❖ It's not until you extinguish the cycles that work against you that you will be able to rediscover who you are and what that means for you. I'm here to tell you that familiarity doesn't necessarily equate to things needing to be permanent.

❖ 3 steps to help you move forward towards eradicating the toxic patterns in your life are:

1. Grow an increasing awareness of what patterns are working against you connecting to where you want to go.
2. Hold yourself accountable. You owe it to yourself. Don't you?
3. Accept that what once was considered your "norm" is now getting in the way of bringing you inner peace.

❖ You are allowed to give yourself permission to break free from the cycles that have kept you feeling like a prisoner. Just because you did it in the past does not mean that it has to remain in your present.

S - Set Boundaries

❖ Boundaries are essential for healthy living when choosing to live your life on purpose. And while setting boundaries is vital to live well, you know what's more important than setting boundaries? Being consistent with them. Standards and Boundaries serve as the "yes's" and "no's" you permit in your life experiences. Providing a succinct definition of what you will and will not allow into your space, allows you to be clear on your needs. It also shows others how they're allowed to interact with you. In essence, you'll have to teach people how to treat you. Let yourself stand firm on what's important to you. Also see: *Be consistent with the boundaries you originally set.*

❖ 4 Things that happen when you start implementing boundaries:

1. You learn to say 'no' to others while saying 'yes' to you.
2. You start doing the things you actually want to do.
3. You begin noticing a decrease of stress and feelings of being overwhelmed.
4. You start taking better care of yourself.

S - Succeed in Being You

❖ When you succeed at being yourself, there's realization that you can show up just as you are without over explaining, justifying, or rationalizing. Success in whatever your goal may be will follow you most when you are showing up authentically. And as you are showing up authentically, make sure you're doing it unapologetically (no shame).

❖ One thing about staying true to you, it is much easier than perpetrating someone else that you're not. May you decide to explore all the ways that lead you back to you.

As an adult who has significantly emotionally matured over the years, I understand that minding my business is essential for living the life I desire. The art of minding your business includes knowing what works for you as well as what does not work for you.

INTENTIONALLY MINDING THE BUSINESS OF ME

If you intentionally took some time right now to take inventory of the business that is you, what will come up for you? Think about your needs, your desires, your prayers and wishes. Who is it that you need to be for those things to come to fruition? Intentionally create an opportunity to reflect on these questions. Use the space provided below to record your thoughts:

_____

_____

_____

_____

_____

_____

_____

_____

_____

_____

_____

_____

_____

The answers that arise will be the business you will need to address. After all, you did pick up this book so you can intentionally mind the business of you. Right?

As you continue to grow interest in enhancing your well-being, developing self-awareness, and gaining tools to get out of your own way, it should become clear that you will have to do the work. The mentally and emotionally thriving version of you is met through doing the work of uncovering, unlearning and relearning things to create better experience for your overall well-being. This is how you cater to your mental wellness. The work is about learning the tools AND then applying those tools.

So, when we talk about minding your business, it's really focusing on all the parts of you. It's making sure your grass is green, your needs are met, and you are showing up in your authenticity. It can be so easy, almost second nature to want to be and do everything for everyone. When we do this, we take away from our very beings. We steal from ourselves and violate ourselves. Yes, not minding and tending to your business, is the ultimate violation of self.

Instead of violating yourself, I welcome you to wholeheartedly embrace yourself. So, quick story but stick with me:

Gardening has become an enjoyable hobby of mine. It's quite therapeutic. Helping me ground, resource, and calm. Through this therapeutic activity, I realize we are not much different than plants in relation to the care, nourishment, attention, and love that is needed to grow and thrive. If plants are not treated well or correctly, they become brittle, dried up and deprived. However, when we tend to our gardens, the soil stays rich, the sun hits just right, the flowers and leaves bloom, there's great energy and a healthy plant commands the room by its presence. Imagine what that plant could look like when tended to well. Beautiful, right? The same can go for you as a human being when you choose to tend to the business of you.

Let's return to the original question that was asked in the beginning of this chapter - We're all going to die; so, what will you do while you're living? If you're still feeling challenged, that's okay. It may be helpful to read the breakdown of the 'Business Framework' again and recall that you are creating new neural pathways in your brain so all new things will take practice to master. Become curious and reflect on how you will make steps to take care of yourself now so you can create a life that connects you with peace and ease. A life that ultimately connects you with the most desired version of you. In summation, this is the foundation to addressing your overall well-being.

Affirmations:

i. I am working on myself and committing to making a difference in my life.

ii. I am welcoming opportunities to care for myself.

iii. I am creating helpful strategies that help me live on purpose.

Take this time to write down any reflections or notes about

Chapter 2: Intentionally Minding the Business of Me.

What are some steps you can take to address your business?

_____

_____

_____

_____

_____

_____

_____

_____

_____

_____

_____

_____

_____

_____

_____

_____

_____

_____

_____

_____

_____

_____

_____

_____

_____

_____

_____

_____

_____

_____

_____

_____

_____

_____

_____

_____

Chapter 3

"May the importance of being good to all of you, not just parts of you, be a space that you revisit over and over again."

- Samiyrah Bennett

Safeguard Your Wellbeing

INTENTIONALLY MINDING THE BUSINESS OF ME

"Don't let anyone rent space in your head, unless they're a good tenant."

Your well-being is directly correlated to your quality of life. When centering on safeguarding your well-being, there is a focus on taking intentional action to protect your wellness.

This life you are living is for You. No matter your other titles like businesswoman, mom, wife, caregiver, etc. Your life is for you. The commonality of all these titles is 'you.' It is incredibly important to put your best foot forward to preserve and protect yourself. Protecting and safeguarding your well-being comprises your social, emotional, physical, financial, environmental, occupational, intellectual, and spiritual wellness. Developing a routine to help meet the needs of all these systems in your life is what it truly looks like to safeguard your well-being. Creating a life you love is your divine right and creating the life connected to your most favorite self will take you caring and pouring into these multiple systems in your life.

When it comes to being intentional about caring for all your systems, it can be challenging. With full transparency, I also have times when I struggle within a certain area. When feeling like you are not meeting the needs of one of your systems, it can be helpful to remind yourself that you are human. Humans make errors and are ever evolving. You're allowed to start where you are and then restart again if needed.

What can be effective while safeguarding your well-being is carrying self-forgiveness with you on this journey. When caring for yourself and meeting the needs of all that's entailed in such, you may begin to be hard on yourself. The next time that you're feeling like you're not doing enough in a certain area, instead of being judgmental of yourself, ask yourself, am I truly doing my best in this area? If the answer is 'yes', then keep practicing your best. Eventually, your best will become even better. If the answer is 'no', connect with the resources you need to help in the area of concern.

Below, you will find the list of the *9 Dimensions of Wellness*. For the context of this reading, I'll be exploring 9 wellness areas with you. Please note that some wellness practitioners argue that there are 8 dimensions of wellness and others state that there are up to 15. For the rest of this reading, we'll focus on 9. While they are all different, they are interconnected to help best support your overall functioning.

Emotional/Mental Wellness: This dimension sheds light on the importance of checking in with how you're feeling. When you feel imbalance, intentionally create awareness about what is coming up for you. Attention is focused on approaching circumstances with the ability to effectively cope with situations presented. Emotional wellness is what leads to ultimate success. Attending therapy can help you enhance your awareness and develop coping skills that promote healthy living. Just as you check in with a doctor, check in with a therapist.

Physical Wellness: Maintain wellness visits, get annual exams, and connect with professionals. Not only when something doesn't feel right. Your physical health has a direct impact on your overall well-being. It's important to get your body moving (physical activity), keep proper nutritional eating habits and get enough rest. Optimal wellness is achieved through healthy habits.

Financial Wellness: Prioritizing your financial health helps you take care of yourself and your family. Financial wellness includes managing your funds and developing new skills to meet your financial needs. Living on purpose includes spending intentionally.

Social Wellness: You are the company that you keep. Be deliberate in your approach in preserving healthy relationships with people. What I've learned throughout my almost 40 years on this earth is that receiving support from people who have your best interest is imperative to living well. May you be encouraged to stay connected to those that make you feel as good as collard greens and cornbread on a Sunday evening. Hmmm, now I'm hungry, but let's keep our attention on the remainder of the Wellness Dimensions.

Environmental Wellness: Create an environment that promotes wellness. Truly define what that looks like for you. How you keep your home, your car, your office space, even your purse can be directly correlated to your mood. Ever notice how you feel slipping into a bed of fresh linens or how you feel after getting in your car after a car wash. For those of you with children, keeping a car clean may be hard to relate to (I know the feeling); so, focus on what you can control. The point is that the places you interact with daily are correlated to your well-being. It's incredibly important to be mindful of your environment in your approach to living well.

Occupational Wellness: The occupational wellness dimension really encompasses how you feel about the work you do in the world. When you're being intentional about your occupational wellness, you create opportunities, you explore what works for you as well as what doesn't. You may find yourself challenged with occupational wellness and yearning to connect with purpose. If this is you, ask yourself, "What do I want to contribute to this world?" or "What difference am I looking to make?" Whatever the answers are to these questions, choose to connect to resources that get you one step closer to living well through your occupation. Stay encouraged to create occupational opportunities doing what you love the most.

Intellectual Wellness: In efforts to support the intellectual aspect of wellness, challenge yourself to get involved in mental activities. Bring curiosity in your approach to stay connected with behaviors that stimulate your mind.

Spiritual Wellness: Grow an increased awareness of your core values and what spirituality means for you. It can range from Religion, Spirituality, Divine, Spirit, Universe to name a few. Being connected to spirituality will also help you connect with purpose, meaning and understanding of your experiences. Taking care of your spiritual wellness will also assist in remaining connected to hope, vision and clarity of needs.

How you care and pay attention to these variety of systems have a direct impact on your quality of life.

Sexual Wellness: Daugherty et. Al (2016) suggests "sexual wellness to be related to sexual satisfaction, mental health and psychosocial variables." Prioritizing your sexual health is aligned with showing loving kindness to your body. Taking good care of yourself includes paying attention to your sexual needs. You're encouraged to engage in sexual experiences that feel safe and allow you to gain thorough understanding of your body's needs. When paying attention to your sexual wellness, autonomy is vital; so, don't be afraid to prioritize yourself whether you're alone or with consenting others.

In efforts to treat your overall self well, it will be imperative to prioritize all dimensions of wellness. Taking true care of yourself would imply that you are taking inventory of the physical, emotional, financial, vocational, spiritual, social, environmental, and intellectual. So, I'll ask again, are you truly taking care of yourself? If the answer is 'no', will you commit to look at one of these dimensions of wellness and decide one way you can start pouring into that area today? Pour into you! Not only do you deserve it but the connection to the most favorite version of you will require it. Your next level will command you to tap in and make improvements in all these areas. I think you can agree that if nothing changes, nothing changes. So, what are you willing to modify so something can finally start changing?

When you are safeguarding your well-being, you are taking care of all of you. Not parts of you here and there but all that encompasses you. The Mind, Body and Soul connection is significant. Our thoughts inform our emotions, which informs our bodies/feelings which in turn connects to our spirit. All our systems work together and if you are deficient in one part of the system then it will couple over to the next system. This becomes a domino effect perpetuating feelings of depletion, exhaustion, and "brokenness." May the importance of being good to all of you, not just parts of you be a space that you revisit over and over again.

Know that you have power! The power that you have is that you get to decide at any minute who you are, what you stand for and how you choose to live your life. When you're doing this, I hope you choose to live on purpose and not have the voices of others dictate who you are. You have been working through survival mode for so long, which can feel quite automatic. Also known as, "going through the motions." I know what that feels like oh too well. In deciding to be intentional about safeguarding your wellness, you'll have to release that 'survival mindset.'

It wasn't until I surrendered to the idea, I no longer have to suffer through survival mode that I was able to truly prioritize my wellness. It's allowed the ability to acknowledge the feelings that are present in my circumstances AND still choose to take inventory of my experience so I can meet the wellness needs of that specific area. Even when it feels uncomfortable. Discomfort is quite difficult to sit in. At times, when experiencing uncomfortable feelings or experiences you may be inclined to put protective guards up.

Keeping your guards up is a natural response as a human living a human experience, especially when facing new approaches to circumstances. Unfortunately, sometimes the guards we have up in attempts to 'block the intruders' end up being the same guards holding us as prisoners of our own circumstances. My question to you: When are you going to allow yourself to be released? The survival mindset needs to be released in order to make room for the mindset that is Thriving!

Affirmations:

i. Checking in with my wellness guides me back to my power and truth.

ii. Taking care of me is my responsibility and I do a very good job.

iii. I deserve to no longer carry people, places and things that are not my responsibility.

Take this time to write down any reflections or notes about

Chapter 3: Safeguarding Your Well Being.

What step can you make now to prioritize your wellness?

Which step will you focus on first?

_____

_____

_____

_____

_____

_____

_____

_____

_____

_____

_____

_____

_____

_____

_____

Chapter 4

"It's time to start exploring and stop storing what is no longer serving you."

- Samiyrah Bennett

Mask Off

"What you can't say owns you. What you hide controls you."

Are you ready to take down your mask or are you still committed to hiding behind the false reality of what you present? The choice is yours. While making the choice, I remind you that you can't heal what you don't reveal.

You may be feeling 'seen' right now. That's ok and it's also the point. As you become more aware and start to 'do the work', you gain insight. This part of the process can be difficult. It's in moving through the discomfort that we can reclaim our power, connect with our authenticity, and truly evolve through the healing journey.

You may be walking around saying that you're "fine" and "ok" when you're carrying around panic, pain, worry, sadness, stress, depression, and/or shame. You may be carrying one, two, all the above or it may be something else that you're carrying. To heal most of these things you must get down to the business of you! We talked about this in Chapter 2. Go back and reference during your reflection of this chapter so you can remember what getting down to the business of you entails. Take a moment to check in with yourself.

Are you being honest with yourself? How you answer that question is important. You must realize that if you decide not to be honest with yourself, you're the only one that has to live with that answer. If you're not honest, you'll be living with that answer and still walking around the same way you've been feeling. You don't feel like that's a lot to carry? The bags aren't too heavy yet? The bags being the emotional baggage that you have been carrying around.

When you choose to ignore what's there and only surface by, you do yourself a disservice. Continuing to suppress your true feelings may feel ok in the moment; but it only exacerbates the problem, making the problem much worse. The act of avoiding feelings, thoughts, and emotions that may cause discomfort or purposefully neglecting these feelings can be identified as emotional suppression. When you hold all these emotions inside, you create internal emotion disruption causing you to feel even more distress and pain. When you deliberately try to forget about painful and unwanted thoughts, it can cause an adverse reaction. The more you want to "forget about it [whatever the 'it' is]", the more it will present itself. The next time you have a thought or emotion that you deem as uncomfortable, don't try to push it away. Instead of trying to impulsively avoid it, practice sitting with it and breathe through it. This paradoxical approach can lead to easing the discomfort and allowing you to process through the discomfort rather than suppressing it.

<u>Paradigm of what occurs when emotions are suppressed</u>

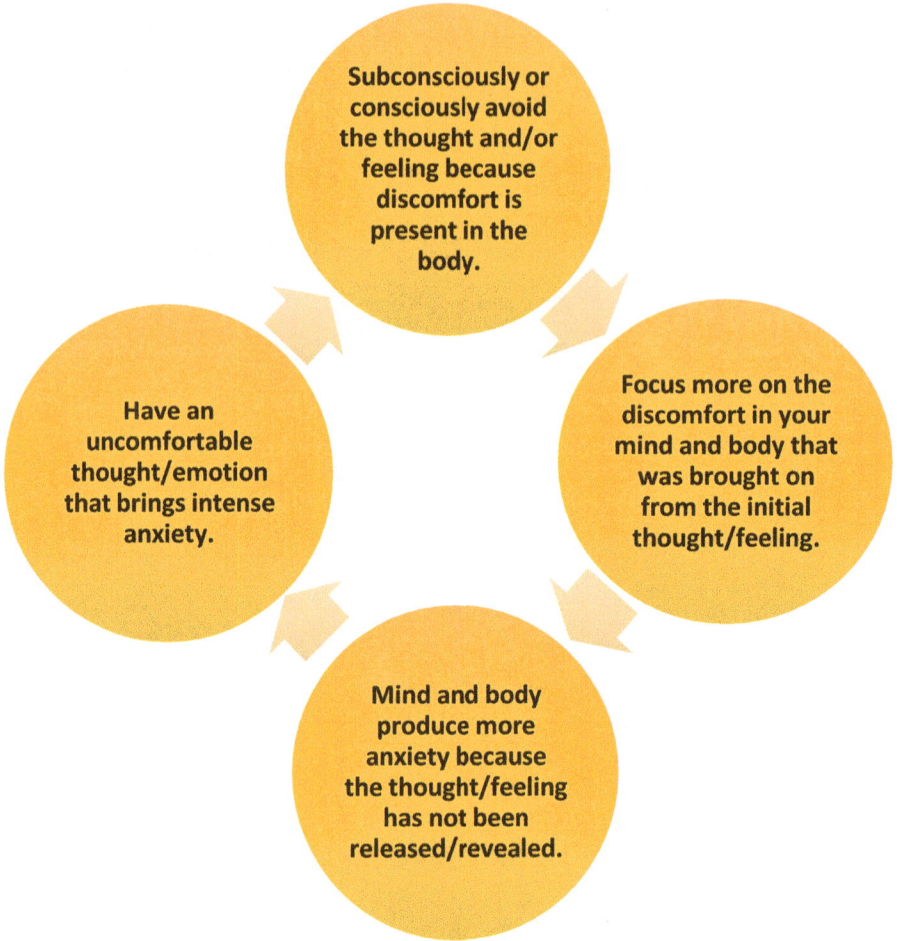

Subconsciously or consciously avoid the thought and/or feeling because discomfort is present in the body.

Focus more on the discomfort in your mind and body that was brought on from the initial thought/feeling.

Have an uncomfortable thought/emotion that brings intense anxiety.

Mind and body produce more anxiety because the thought/feeling has not been released/revealed.

And this is how a negative cycle of emotional suppression is created.

A healthy alternative:

Next time an uncomfortable thought or feeling comes, acknowledge it. Take a deep breath - inhale through your nose and exhale through your mouth. Picture the thought or feeling as a wave at the beach. You are the sand, and the uncomfortable feeling/thought is the wave. Let the thought (wave) come up and as it comes over the sand (you), allow its presence. Then, imagine the thought being released from you as the wave leaves the sand and travels back to low tide.

Note: This exercise may feel a bit ridiculous at first because it may be a different practice than what you are used to. However, with practice you will become more comfortable.

Try this exercise out with emotions and thoughts that do not feel so overwhelming at first. The more you practice with the 'little things', you can then apply this exercise to the 'big things.'

Through it all, I welcome you to stop acting like you're good all the time. As an individual living the human experience, it's impossible to be good all the time. So, when you have these feelings, it is best to embrace them. Sit with the feelings whether uncomfortable or not so you can provide opportunity to process through it rather than suppressing it.

Can I be transparent with you?

Thank you.

I know exactly how it feels to be a prisoner of your mind. To experience self-doubt, serious depressive thoughts, high anxiety, and panic. Yup, that's right! Even the healer requires healing, too. After acknowledging that something was off and gaining interest in doing something about it, I realized it would be best to speak about what was occurring instead of holding it in. With exploring helpers that may be able to provide support and guidance, came shame and some serious self-judgment. After all, I am the one that is supposed to be helping everyone else. How can I admit that I am experiencing challenges, too? It wasn't until there was space to reveal my internal experience that there was the ability to successfully manage it all using healthy coping skills. I reveal this because I want you to know that you are not alone in your circumstance.

Most people experience some level of mental health disturbances at one period of their lives or another. However, everyone is not honest about their feelings and choose to forever hide behind the mask. If you don't take anything else away from this section, I want to reiterate that it's not about what you experience, it's about what you decide to do about it so you can function in a healthier way.

Something was truly wrong. I felt off and even started to experience some psychosomatic symptoms. Psychosomatic symptoms are when you have physical symptoms that are directly correlated to your emotional state with no clear medical cause. I was ashamed AND I didn't want to feel like that any longer. So, what did I do? I explored meeting with a therapist. The therapist got a therapist to help me unpack and it changed the trajectory of my life.

Therapy provides a safe space where you no longer need to wear the mask. It was and is a place where I can be vulnerable, transparent, and unleash all the thoughts and emotions that I may not want anyone else to see or hear. Once I began revealing, there was a conscious notation of how good I felt after each session. I got to walk away lighter, more liberated, and with gained clarity.

Sometimes when it is just you and your thoughts, it can make you feel like you are alone. Because if you're not speaking it, you're storing it. Again, if you are not speaking it, you're storing it. Storing it typically leads to emotional suppression and that can affect your entire system. Will you decide to explore ways to make peace with the war happening in your internal world? Explore more ways to connect with peace? Deciding to hold on to your inner conflicts will lead to an array of mental health issues and challenges. These issues and challenges include, but are not limited to, depression, anxiety, hallucinations, panic, delusions, irritability, and/or high stress levels.

Not revealing what you're experiencing leads to you living in your head, which keeps you from living life on purpose. You're prevented from living the life you deserve and were destined to live.

Many people believe that they must figure it out all by themselves. If they share what they experience internally, no one will understand. Once you make the choice to keep everything in and internalize, it causes more harm to your internal systems and outside world. You end up battling yourself. Literally going to war with yourself. What has been apparent in my life's work is that as humans, we don't heal in isolation. Expressing your experience to others provides an opportunity for you to realize that many other people may be feeling the same way that you do. And if they're not currently feeling that way it may have been an experience that they can relate to because they felt that way in the past. You heal in community and with others. Therefore, it's important to reveal what your experience is so that you can truly heal by releasing what's holding you hostage.

I am aware that the mere thought of expressing your deepest thoughts and feelings can be scary. After all, you have held onto them for so long. Speaking about them, may bring up fear, shame, disgust, and doubt. The fact that you can't heal what you don't reveal should enlighten you to understand that you are doing yourself an incredible disservice by keeping it all in. As the super talented, Lauryn Hill lyrically expounded on the album titled, Miseducation of Lauryn Hill, "How you gonna win when you ain't right within" (Hill, 1998).

Ask yourself, how can I expect to excel when I'm not fully honest with what I am experiencing? If you were to dive within and remove the mask that you continuously present to other people, what will you find there? Who is that person? That mask that you wear so often, it's used to help protect you, so you may think. At the same time, that mask is also keeping you away from meeting the favorite version of you that you're yearning to get closer to.

Now, I'm not saying to start going around telling everyone about everything that you are carrying. You are encouraged to get curious about connecting with a helper, advisor, therapist, coach, spiritual leader, etc. that you feel safe with so you can start exploring and stop storing what is no longer serving you.

Let's be honest, the reason why you can't begin your healing journey is because you're walking around faking the funk. I'm here to tell you that going with the motions and acting like nothing is wrong will only leave you stagnant. Yup, choosing to not reveal when you need help or rejecting help will rob you from your healing. Trust me. I know. Remember what I shared? It wasn't until I decided to get real with myself and what I was experiencing that I started to see major transformations in my life and my feelings. It wasn't until I *stopped* lying telling myself that I wasn't going through anything and that I had to be the strong one is when transformations happened. The next level towards connecting to the more desired version of you, requires surrendering to the fact that your internal world is falling apart. Don't be fooled into thinking that revealing your internal struggles makes you weak when, in fact, it is the total opposite. It's extremely courageous, brave, and self-loving.

You keep wondering why you are feeling like no matter what you do, you remain in the same place. You make vision boards; you read self-help books; and keep up with the latest motivational speaker. So, why are you having a difficult time moving forward in your personal journey? Could it be that all those things are external factors and you're avoiding doing the real work on self? Again, you'll have to be honest with yourself in your answer.

What I know for certain is that you'll be stuck in the cycle of surviving if you continue to pretend that everything is ok, if deep down you are hurting and feeling like you are falling apart. What would happen if you put in the work so you can thrive and live life intentionally?

Earlier, we discussed breaking toxic patterns. Making the decision to not reveal things that may be burdening you is a pattern that is toxic to your overall well-being. The more you hold on to it, the more you prolong your suffering. Can I invite you to take your mask off? While healing is ever evolving, taking the first step of acknowledging that there is a mask that needs to be taken down and then purposefully deciding to do something about it is a step forward in your healing journey.
It's time to take your mask off so that you can reveal what's truly there and begin healing. Remember, you can't heal what you don't reveal. Mask off!

Affirmations:

i.   I am making room for my feelings and emotions.

ii.   I release judgment and stand in my truth.

iii. I am committed to supporting the parts of me that I've kept hidden for too long.

Take this time to write down any reflections or notes about

Chapter 4: Mask Off.

What are you going to admit that you are feeling challenged by?

What resource(s) are you going to connect with to meet your needs?

_____

_____

_____

_____

_____

_____

_____

_____

_____

_____

_____

_____

_____

_____

Chapter 5

"When it comes to moving out of your own way, you'll have to ask yourself, what role am I playing in my own suffering?"

- Samiyrah Bennett

Move Out of Your Own Way

INTENTIONALLY MINDING THE BUSINESS OF ME

You are far too smart to be the only thing standing in your way.

-Jennifer J. Freeman

One of the fastest ways to connect with your most favorite self does include taking inventory of what's in your way. I am here to tell you that, sometimes, the thing that is mostly in your way is YOU.

Maybe it's a toxic behavior that you continuously engage in, unhealthy patterns that keep you in a vicious cycle or not trusting yourself to show up authentically. Whatever it is, there will be a point in your journey where you'll have to stop pointing the finger at every external source. Your healing journey will need you to make room to look within. You're invited to welcome a growing awareness of self and choose to hold yourself accountable on your personal journey. After all, if your goal is developing and excelling, you'll have to acknowledge what role you play in helping you reach new heights.

I know, I know. You're probably like, "OK! Stop yelling at me!" I realize having to admit that you may be the one that is in your own way is challenging. Personally, I understand what it feels like to be looking at everyone and everything around you and expecting things to change. It wasn't until I took a deep look within, understood my worth, listened to my needs and accepted that no one was coming to save me that I was able to take the next step. The next step was taking accountability for my part and once I started to define what my part was, the game changed!

For some, it may not be what you need to do but what you need to stay away from. There are certain things, people, and places that are currently a part of your experience that YOU KNOW are not in your best interest. You are aware that these very things are harmful to your mental wellness, emotional well-being, as well as your physical and spiritual self. Yet and still, you continue to get entangled in them. This is what holds you back from elevating. Continuing to do what you have always done, will never get you different results. In addition, surrounding yourself with the things you need to be freed from, will never allow you to live a purposeful life. Instead, it will continue to weigh you down.

What was that? Oh, it seems, Self-Sabotage has entered the chat. That's right. Consciously understanding what you should be doing and having the will, yet persistently going against what's best for you is a form of sabotaging yourself.

Let's pause for an exercise. I want you to take your right hand and slowly put down all your fingers except one. This may be your index finger or another finger that you are more comfortable with; however, there's going to be one finger that's up. Slowly point to something that is in the room or wherever you are right now. After spending 30 seconds focusing on the object that you chose, I want you to slowly move your finger away from that object and have it start to face you.

This exercise reminds you that no matter how long you decide to focus on the external source it may not change. However, you are in the driver seat of moving your finger and deciding what you'll focus on next. This will help change the trajectory of your experience. Are you ready to focus on you and the way you may need to modify behaviors to truly meet the most favorite version of you? You get to choose what you are willing to focus on and for how long. You get to decide when you are ready to move out of your own way.

With a readiness to step towards moving out of your own way, take fast action!

Check out these 7 strategies to begin decreasing self-sabotaging behavior:

1.   *Know that self-sabotage will present itself.* Instead of being judgmental when it arises, offer yourself compassion. It may be helpful to be reflective and ask, "Why am I doing (_____) when I know it is not in my best interest." Be honest in your answer.

2.   *Limit self-criticism.* You'll meet more than enough people who will try to go against you in your life. No need to add to that list by going against yourself. Embrace where you are AND where you want to go.

3.   *Collaborate with a Mental Health Therapist.* A therapist will help you see parts of the picture that you may not be able to see on your own. Getting the support of an unbiased person will assist in expanding your awareness and insight into your circumstance. The process will help you get to the root of your self-sabotaging behavior.

4.   *Establish S.M.A.R.T.* Goals that are attainable for you and your circumstance. In efforts to set yourself up for success, you'll want to make sure your goals are *Specific, Measurable, Attainable, Realistic* and have a *Time Frame.*

5.   *Start Small.* It's not about doing everything at one time. There should be more regard for what needs to be accomplished *first.*

6.   *Set Standards that support Healthy Living.* What does living a healthy life mean to you? Do the people, places, and things you surround yourself with fall into this definition or go against it? If it is the latter, take inventory and make necessary steps to remove what doesn't fit into your criteria to live well.

7.   *Refrain from People Pleasing patterns.* This journey is yours. If you are fixated on pleasing the needs of everyone else, you continue to steal

the opportunity to meet your needs. Bring intentional focus to the only person you have control of truly making happy: yourself.

Oftentimes, the people who find themselves in their own way are the ones who keep putting other people, places, and things before themselves. What would happen if I told you that the change you're seeking can't reveal itself because you're not prioritizing yourself? When is the last time you've been true to you and your needs? Once identifying those needs, have you followed through on meeting them?

Listen, when you are doing something different than your mind and body are used to, self-doubt and insecurity will feel like they have an open invitation into your journey. Just because they show up, it does not mean that you have to offer them a plate to eat. You know what I mean? Stand firm in your health and wellness goals. Prepare to eliminate anything that doesn't align.

When it comes to moving out of your own way, you'll have to ask yourself, what role am I playing in my own suffering? It may be who you choose to hang out with, what you choose to consume or refusing to say what you really want to say with fear that you may be judged. The role you play in your own suffering may also look like procrastinating to get a therapist or wellness coach. It's time to take accountability for the role you play.

Taking accountability for your actions can be difficult. Especially when you are not accustomed to doing so. However, in efforts to modify behaviors that prevent us from being stagnant, it's imperative to own your part. Ultimately, moving out of your comfort zone. Your elevated version is not waiting for you in your comfort zone. Once you decide to stop blocking yourself from connecting with your most favorite version of you, there will be some requirements. This includes setting intentions, remaining curious, being present, investing in yourself, choosing to love yourself, as well as others, and be purposeful in your actions. When you make a conscious decision to only be fueled by what allows you to grow, the game changes exponentially.

Writing these words is taking me to a place when I personally had to move out of my own way. Literally, right before I finally sat down and decided to write this book. Writing literature to encourage wellness has been heavy on my heart for some time now. I kept putting it off. And then, I kept putting it off some more. Telling myself so many different narratives. Just making up all kinds of things "in my head." I was telling myself the narratives of "it's not going to be good enough" and "no one is going to read it." I was also thinking, "I don't have time to write a book." Reflection and curiosity had me then ask, "Is it that I don't have time or was I not prioritizing it?" As you can see, the answer was the latter.

The more I put it off, the more I realized I was postponing my excellence. Postponing a purposeful approach to further connect with my most favorite self. How dare I betray myself like that? I had to move out of my own way to produce a body of work that would be life changing for another human to read. I share that to remind you that it's not how you start but all about the journey/process and how you finish. It's also shared to remind you that no matter who you are, you are not removed from experiencing self-defeating thoughts. As I so often explain to many of my clients, it's not about the thoughts not coming to you. Overcoming is more about how we manage and the skills we use to conquer those thoughts that arise.

In the process of getting out of your own way, I ask that you move towards engaging in transformative work. Keep asking, keep evolving, keep moving, and keep shining. Regardless of the change you'll have to make to become the greatest version of you, it is worth exploring. You deserve the very least of discovering what that might look like for you. The version of you that you're so yearning to meet, wants to meet you, too.

At some point, you'll have to stop leaning on the excuses of why it's not working. Instead, you're encouraged to get out of your own way and tap into the resources to find out how it can work, ultimately, moving from a fixed mindset to a growth mindset. A fixed mindset avoids challenges and will tell you things like, "I can't do hard things because I might fail." While a growth mindset will say that "great things take time AND effort. I'm capable of completing one task at a time." You're capable! That same capability will also require both willingness and desire to be fully effective.

Although your thoughts are not facts, the way you speak to yourself daily has a big impact on your life. The first chapter 'Affirmations' mentioned how your brain is always recording; so, you're encouraged to be very mindful of what you are repeating to yourself. May you begin fostering an environment that nurtures and grooms your inner dialogue. This will take practice. If you feel overwhelmed by the inner dialogue, it may be best to link with a mental health professional. As an advocate for mental health, you'll read this reminder all throughout this book: you do not have to walk your journey alone.

While challenges may present themselves to you, it is your responsibility and business to take charge in your life. You get to move. You get to change things up at any time. You get to take control. To move out of your own way is to release yourself from self-sabotaging behaviors, stagnation, self-neglect and abandonment of your core values. All emotions that will leave you feeling broken. My hope is that you incorporate tools and skills that prepare you for your breakthrough.

Recognize your accomplishments, your efforts, and your interest in becoming, evolving, and thriving as you travel on your personal healing journey. You deserve the restoration waiting for you as you give yourself what you need. Are you ready to tap into your divine self? Let's practice some affirmations that can help you stop blocking your greatness.

Affirmations:

i. Getting through challenging things in the past is evidence that I can get through this difficult time.

ii. I deserve to be honest with myself and what I need.

iii. I am open to learning how to support myself.

iv. I am committed to connecting to resources that help me move out of my own way.

v. My divine self is waiting for me to take the next step that's in my best interest.

Take this time to write down any reflections or notes about

Chapter 5: Move Out of Your Own Way.

Name 5 ways you are going to hold yourself accountable to get out of

your way. What are the steps that you need to make? Starting today!

_____

_____

_____

_____

_____

_____

_____

_____

_____

_____

_____

_____

_____

_____

_____

_____

Chapter 6

"What matters most is how you handle NOW, for the past has moved forward and the future has not arrived yet."

- Samiyrah Bennett

Embrace the Present Moment

"Accept, then Act. Whatever the present moment contains, accept it as if you have chosen it. Always work with it, not against it."

- Eckhart Tolle

Embrace the Present Moment -

Our society has perpetuated a notion that to be successful, you must always be busy. For me, the definition of success is to be connected with peace. Top tier peace is met when you intentionally create opportunities to live in the here and now.

While working in the mental health field, my observations have been that many people live their lives being too far in the past or way ahead in the future. The harm in this approach of living is that when we ruminate on the past, we foster an experience that promotes regret, worry, depression, and stress. Living in the future promotes anxiety and feelings of being overwhelmed and 'stuck.'

Making a purposeful decision to embrace the present moment provides an opportunity to move from having a 'mind full' to being mindful. When your mind is full, you'll find yourself experiencing chaos, brain fog, and inability to actively listen. This results in increased worry and high anxiety. On the other hand, when you are creating a mindful atmosphere, you are intentionally paying particular attention to the present moment. Engaging in the act of Mindfulness can be helpful when choosing to live a life that connects you to more peace.

Mindfulness is a therapeutic practice where you pay particular attention to the present moment, focusing on one thing without judgment. Quan et. al (2018) explains practicing mindfulness guides people to take a relatively positive attitude toward all thoughts and sounds that intrudes one's life. The breath is a good place to start when beginning to practice mindfulness. Let's try it right now.

Focus on the rhythmic pattern of your breath. Notice how your chest rises and falls.

Without trying to change the pattern, simply notice how your heart and lungs are doing exactly what they need to do for you.

Thank them and observe how the air feels as you breathe in through your nose and out of your mouth.

Allow all questions or thoughts that arise to come and simply watch them go as you bring yourself back to this moment in time.

A moment where you are doing something just for you.

Taking notice of how your body is supporting you.

Breathe in through your nose, counting to 4, hold your breath for 2 and then elongate the exhale for 6.

Breathe.

Repeat 4 times.

Congratulations, you just completed a mindfulness practice!

As you travel through your life journey, one thing will remain consistent: your life will be filled with moments. Because of this, it is important to live moment by moment. All you have right now is this moment. Nothing else is a priority at this time, for when something else arises, it will be that moment. Stay right here, right now. Allowing yourself to just breathe.

Benefits of engaging in Mindfulness exercises include decreased anxiety and stress, more love and self-compassion, improved self-awareness, as well as increased patience and productivity. Overall, mindfulness helps you to intentionally pay attention while carrying a non-judgmental approach. It can be helpful to incorporate acts of mindfulness daily. An example of this would be instead of rushing through lunch, you carve out time to notice what you're eating, how it feels in your mouth and truly enjoy the taste of all the ingredients. This is truly being present: moving in the here and now. The act of mindfulness helps you to approach your experience with curiosity rather than fear. Further, mindfulness assists you in attaining self-regulation as you can often feel overstimulated when your mind is full.

Slowing down for moments at a time can make quite a difference in your life and make you more productive than being oversaturated with work and constantly doing. For me, personally, I've noticed a drastic difference in my life, in my mood, and in my overall functioning since shifting from a life of doing, doing, doing to now allowing myself to "be."

When you are not living in the moment, you will find yourself too focused on the future or ruminating on the past. Rumination can be described as having consistent thoughts that typically focus on a problem or situation on repeat in your mind. In this context, living in the future is not regarding goal planning. We want to plan for our future and set ourselves up for success. However, it becomes problematic when you're preoccupied with the future and consistently worry about the 'what ifs.'

Just as being goal oriented about what lies ahead can be a healthy way of focusing on the future, reflection of the past is also beneficial. Although helpful, reflection becomes problematic when it shifts to dwelling. Once you find yourself dwelling on past or future events, this is identified as rumination as well. The concept of rumination is most often identified with mental health challenges such as anxiety and depression. Being fixated on the 'what ifs' and 'what was' leads to spiraling thoughts that contribute to an overactive mind.

If you find yourself experiencing heightened anxiety, frustration, worry, and stress, I welcome you to create space between your thoughts and the present moment. Here are a couple of ways that you can intentionally establish connection with the present moment:

❖ Refrain from criticizing self for the thoughts experienced. Whether negative or positive, thoughts come. Suffering can transpire when there is over identification with the specific thought that has presented itself. Remind yourself that you are a human that's having a human experience.

❖ Choose to see your thoughts, not be your thoughts. Welcome a non-judgmental approach by becoming an observer of your thoughts instead of being engrossed by your thoughts.

❖ Acknowledge your thoughts and then let them wave on by. An uncomfortable thought comes, notice it, and give yourself permission to release it. Allowing yourself to have a moment for the thought to pass will help release the tension of resisting and lead you to work with your thoughts by embracing them and not fighting against them by using resistance.

❖ Stay present by asking yourself, "What do I need to do to support myself in this moment?" Bring loving attention to what you are in control of at this moment.

With the ability to improve mood, reduce racing thoughts and decrease anxiety and depression, my hope is that you begin to embrace the present moment. To know while things have occurred and other things will happen, what matters most is how you handle what's presenting itself now. For the past has moved forward and the future has not arrived yet. When the future does get here, it will in fact be the present moment. My hope is that you commit to choosing what's in your best interest for right now.

Affirmations

    i.   I am not too old, and it is not too late.

    ii.   I choose to live in the only moment that I have at this time, the present moment.

   iii.   I release the chains of the past and bring particular attention to what I need at this moment.

   iv.   I choose to live *NOW*.

Take this time to write down any reflections or notes about

Chapter 6: Embrace the Present Moment.

Name 3 ways how you are going to be intentionally present.

_____

_____

_____

_____

_____

_____

_____

_____

_____

_____

_____

_____

_____

_____

_____

_____

_____

Chapter 7

"One thing for sure is that relationships take work. That includes the relationship with yourself."

- Samiyrah Bennett

Care & Preservation of Self. A Birth Rite.

INTENTIONALLY MINDING THE BUSINESS OF ME

"Self-Care is not Self-Indulgence. It is Self-Preservation."

- Audre Lorde

As a therapist I find myself having many conversations with individuals revolving around self-care. Typically, when I first ask the question, "How do you care for yourself?", the answers revolve around external methods. Methods include going to the spa, manicures and pedicures, bath routine with essential oils, etc. While all are truly relaxing experiences of calm that we should incorporate in our lives, I want to be clear that is not all self-care entails.

Here, we're going to talk about how self-care is more than mani, pedis and retail therapy. Self-care that is radical in nature encompasses all of you. Not just the surface. Are you ready to stop dealing with yourself only at surface value? The business of intently caring for yourself includes paying particular attention to overall mental and emotional wellness. As you can see, caring for self and ensuring self-preservation is a multi-faceted approach.

In efforts to expand on the concept of self-care and fully embrace this approach, let's take the opportunity to review some other ways one may indulge in self-care. Here's what that may look like:

Establishing Boundaries

❖ In Chapter 2, we discussed Intentionally Minding the Business of You, which included boundaries. So, let's review. When we create boundaries, we support self-preservation. Why is this? Because we deliberately take inventory of those things that are in our best interest. This can ultimately protect you from people, places, and things that compromise you connecting with your most favorite self.

Being consistent with Boundaries

❖ As we stated before, we not only want to set boundaries, but we want to be consistent with them. You'll notice when you become consistent with the boundaries that are right for your life, other people will modify the way that they approach you. This is because they are no longer able to interact with you in the ways that they were before. In turn, being consistent with these boundaries will help you create healthy relationships, manage your stress and anxiety that may be present, as well as safeguarding your well-being like we talked about in Chapter 3.

❖ What you also want to remember is that when you implement healthy boundaries, people around you will be resistant to respecting them. Let's just say this is the case at first. Caring for yourself means being consistent with your boundaries despite the discomfort it may cause for others. And trust me, other people will get very uncomfortable about the boundaries that you set. It does not mean that your boundary is wrong, it means that those individuals will have to adjust in the way they interact with you. Know that this is OK. You're setting boundaries to care for, help, preserve and uplift yourself. Doing what's in your best interest is your birthright.

Going to Therapy

❖ Going to therapy is one of the top ways that you can show ultimate care for yourself and for your well-being. As humans, we go through so many things throughout the day, throughout the month, throughout years that we hold onto. If I'm honest, moment by moment on some days.

❖ When you're committed to the process of living life on purpose, you will most likely yearn to think, act, and do something different. Eventually, developing new patterns to approach your life experience. Therapy allows you to understand you do not have to create these new patterns by yourself.

❖ Furthermore, therapy teaches you to take a step back, become aware of exactly what you need, and formulate tangible ways that you can meet your needs on purpose. It's truly a path that leads you to improved insight and self-discovery. Now, THAT'S what I call taking care of yourself! Being connected to the right therapist for you can provide clarification that you no longer have to do what you've been doing that has kept you feeling stagnant while also offering strategies to take the alternative path desired. Once you are attending therapy and consistently doing the work, you will find yourself caring and loving yourself in ways that you never could even imagine. Ultimately, falling in love with your most favorite self more and more.

Eating Well

❖ Eating well has a direct correlation to your mind and bodily functions. So, it makes sense that when we are mindful about our food intake, it has an impact on our emotional, mental, and physical self. Caring for ourselves is making sure we're eating well so that we can live well.

❖ Eating well balanced meals can improve your mood, increase your memory and brain health, and improve overall functioning.

Utilizing Healthy Coping Skills

❖ Utilizing healthy coping skills insinuates that when you are faced with a challenge, you don't automatically go to what may be damaging and harmful towards you. Instead, you go towards action steps that take in consideration of connecting with your most favorite self. After all, that is the goal that we are after.

Right? The goal of continuing to evolve, thrive, and heal on purpose.

❖ A couple of ways to foster healthy coping skills are to be intentional about rest and practice an attitude of gratitude. I'd also encourage you to be mindful of who you allow into your space/presence while creating experiences that directly connect you to laughter and joy.

After reading that, can you honestly say that you are indulging in self-care that feeds all your systems? If not, what is one way that you are now committed to taking care of yourself?

What I know for certain is that relationships take work. That includes the relationship with yourself. I invite you to really get serious about the way you care for yourself and the work you implement to truly connect with your inner self. Begin to become curious about who you are and all the ways that you can care for you. You'll begin to expand your mindset. Additionally, connecting with your inner self will help to support your mental health and explore roadblocks that leave you with a feeling of being 'stuck.' This is the work that helps you manage what comes up so you can experience an improved mood rather than just saying you're okay.

Saying you're ok and that you're good does not make the pain go away. It does not magically erase the root of the problem. The only thing that "saying you're okay when you're really not" does is prolong your ability and opportunity to heal. In contrast, if you pause to identify the true feelings, you get the chance to gain awareness of your needs and process them ON PURPOSE.

So, the next time that you're quick to say, "I'm ok", I invite you to really explore your feelings. You may find instead of "ok", you may also feel out of control, amazed, insecure, jealous, disappointed, courageous, thankful or another truer emotion tucked away under the surface. It's not until you get honest with yourself and what your true needs are that you can live the life you deserve. Until you meet yourself with radical honesty, you will continuously do yourself a disservice. The disservice comes when you only gratify the surface.

For the nature of this book, when we're talking about self-care it's about caring for your soul. It's about exploring ways to best meet your true internal needs, beyond the surface.

Outside of the manicures and pedicures we were talking about earlier, self-care can also come in the form of blocking, ignoring, deleting, and unfollowing. It's okay if someone or something just popped into your head as you read that. This confirms there's an awareness of where you want to be headed and that person or thing doesn't fit into that version of you. Grant yourself permission to let go of the things that do not fuel your best interest. Being intentional about what you consume and allow into your environment is vital.

Most times your healing journey will not look like how you pictured it. When it gets most challenging is when it's best to stay the path. Your abundance and glow up is on the other side. It is that very reason why I encourage you to connect with resources that make room for you to persevere and push through what may be uncomfortable. Just because your experience on your wellness journey feels uncomfortable, it doesn't mean that it's wrong. It is unfamiliar, and you will have to learn to get out of your comfort zone so that you can get something different. Engaging in new practices can help foster a deeper act of care for self.

As previously mentioned, radical self-care will encompass tools for the Mind, Body, and Spirit. Try some of these examples to start.

Self-Care for Mind examples:

- ❖ Journal/brain dump. The goal will be for you to get everything out of your head and onto a piece of paper so that you can organize the thoughts that are arising, clarify what needs to be released, and prioritize what requires attention first.
- ❖ Disconnect from social media and all other distracting technology.
- ❖ Practice a State of Mindfulness every day.

Self-Care for Body examples:

- ❖ Rest! - This is something you're welcomed to prioritize. Spoiler alert: You do not have to be doing all of the things all of the time.
- ❖ Stay hydrated.
- ❖ Move your body through dance, yoga, or exercise.

Self-Care for Spirit examples:

- ❖ Forgive yourself. The best way to release yourself from past traumatic events is to offer self-forgiveness. As a reminder, you made the best decision you could have with the knowledge you had at that time.
- ❖ Create open mindedness and a receiving heart to explore spirituality and what that means for you.
- ❖ Engage in daily practices of intentionality and gratitude.
- ❖ Spend time in prayer and stillness.
- ❖ Listen to spiritual and calming music.

It's important to reiterate that all our systems work hand in hand. So that means that when one system is off, it pulls from the other systems. If you are neglecting the true work of building up your systems, the entire system of you becomes unmotivated, depleted, and burned out.

Professionally and personally, I will always advocate for seeking and connecting with a Mental Health provider as one of the greatest ways to take care of yourself.

Listen, life gets challenging. That we know for sure. As a human being, you experience multiple moments in your life where you may feel that you don't know how you are going to move to the next. Sometimes it can even feel like you're breaking down. While it's understood that having these occurrences are inevitable in life, I want to normalize that feeling this way sometimes is part of the human experience. This means it is vital to give yourself permission to have a moment but just know that the moment doesn't have to be your final destination.

Knowing that a moment doesn't have to be your final destination truly resonates with me. This is how I've lived my life since I was a child. My mother always used to say to my sister and I, "It's okay to have a moment (meltdown, cry, etc.) but don't stay there - find your way back to your happy place." Taking care of ourselves and always "getting back in focus" has been a lifestyle.

While this has been a part of my story and conditioning, I'm sharing with you what I know for sure: LIFE happens! Through it, there will be valleys and pits, and, AT THE SAME TIME, there will also be peaks and highs. If you provide the opportunity to check in with yourself during your "lows" and allow yourself to not only have the moment but fully process what is occurring, it can completely change the way you experience life.

You're reading this book because you're interested in changing the trajectory. Well, let's check in. You are interested in enhancing your wellness skills to change the trajectory, right? Know that developing a different outcome to stressful situations starts with you.

So here are the steps:

1. **Experiencing a low moment:** Release the Emotion(s).
2. **Check-in:** Name the emotion that's presenting itself.
3. **Process:** Why might this feeling be coming up? Is it something that requires a solution right away?
4. **Refocus:** What do you need at this moment? (A hug, to talk, to scream, walk, time?)
5. **Plan:** I'm going to connect with _____ in order to meet this need. (Self, friend, therapist, spouse, exercise, nature, etc.)
6. **Prioritize:** What's in your best interest to do next?

What would life look like for you if you decided to give your very best to the ones you loved? What if you chose to give your loved ones the very best of you instead of what is left of you? If this intrigues you, understand that in being able to provide the very best, you'll have to take care of yourself. Since you may be looking at self-care from a new lens now, I welcome you to start prioritizing your care and wellness so that you can start breaking toxic patterns.

Another major way to prioritize your care is by providing yourself with mental health days. Notice I said provide yourself. Taking a Mental Health Day is creating intentional time to take inventory of your needs and provide yourself with the resources to meet said need. Mental Health days are vital for functioning well. Take inventory and notice what you need. That job, that event, that circumstance, it's going to be there. But if you don't take care of yourself, it's a high probability that you won't be here. So, I need you to prioritize your mental health needs which is essentially prioritizing you.

While others may consider mental health days as an adult time out, I really consider mental health days as time in. Time IN! Time in with yourself, time in with your needs, time in with your emotions, time in with understanding of self, time in with self-compassion, time in with self-care, and time in with self-love.

You deserve time with yourself so you can live well and function at a capacity to meet your most favorite version. I want you to not only normalize mental health days but prioritize them. You cannot continue attending to the external factors in your life if you're not attending to yourself.

Reach out for help when you know that you need it. What a wonderful way that you can show yourself some love and care. Sometimes you can't do it on your own. Know that you don't have to do it on your own. Any way you feel like you're struggling, there is someone or something that can assist you in getting to the next level towards your goal. It will require you to be vulnerable, to be transparent and determined to get what you want.

Ask for help! Are you feeling like you're struggling mentally and emotionally? Get a therapist. Feeling like you need to be surrounded by different networks and to just be exposed to people who are already in the positions of where you want to go? Get a Mentor. Feeling like you want to scale your business? Get a business coach. You don't have to figure it all out on your own. Explore ways that you can care for and preserve yourself. Live life on purpose! Now, that's radical self-care. Connecting with yourself by all means and in all ways.

Affirmations:

i.   I am learning to take great care of myself.

ii.   I am open to new ways to care for me.

iii.   My self-care is worth making time for.

Take this time to write down any reflections or notes about

Chapter 7: Care & Preservation of Self.

Script out how you are going to care for yourself on purpose.

_____

_____

_____

_____

_____

_____

_____

_____

_____

_____

_____

_____

_____

_____

_____

_____

_____

"Everyday you're provided with an opportunity to explore ways you can love yourself a little more than yesterday."

- Samiyrah Bennett

Let Love Flow On You & Through You

Self-love:

Unconditional positive

self-regard

As a long-time student of psychology, I have encountered the work of Carl Rogers many times. Carl Rogers, a humanistic psychologist expanded the work of having an "unconditional positive regard" for clients when working in the mental health field. Having an unconditional positive regard for clients means expressing complete acceptance, support, care, love, and empathy towards them. The concept of unconditional positive regard is surfacing at this time because I truly believe it is a practice that everyone should demonstrate towards themselves. To fully accept, support, care and show empathy towards self is the ultimate form of self-love.

"I must undertake to love myself and to respect myself. Respect myself as though my very life depends upon self-love and self-respect."

- Maya Angelou

As the aforementioned quote written so eloquently by Maya Angelou expresses, it would be in your best interest to prioritize self-love and self-respect like your life depends on it. Yes, your life does depend on it! If you don't know how to love yourself or how worthy you are of love, it will be impossible to teach others about the way you require love. Loving you is a requirement to living well. It's important that your self-love is stronger than your desire to receive love from someone else. When you decide to intentionally love yourself, it provides an opportunity for you to gain awareness of what works for you and what doesn't. It will also allow the ability to teach others how to show love while allowing you to express love more freely. After all you are going to have to teach people how to love you and how are you gonna be able to do that when you don't know how to love yourself?

Fully embodying self-love will require you to prioritize your needs. It will be essential for you to put yourself first. To be clear, putting yourself first doesn't mean that you are neglecting everyone else. It simply means that you have moved yourself up on the ranking ladder. It means that you are finally not willing to compromise your sense of self for someone else's comfort. Some people believe that participating in radical self-love is a form of selfishness. According to the Merriam-Webster dictionary, self-love is defined as "an appreciation of one's own worth or value" (n.d.). So, you tell me. Is it important for you to acknowledge your worth and value? At this moment, as you're reading this, I want you to give yourself permission. Permission to unapologetically love yourself.

Repeat after me: I choose to love myself not for anyone else but for me. For it is after I show myself love that I am able to love others without depleting me.

What I have learned through my journey thus far is that self- love isn't vanity. Self-love is indeed sanity. Engaging in self-love brings an increase of peace, joy, kindness, and care to your inner self. When you allow love to flow on you and through you, you present the ability to enhance clarity, understanding, and connection with you.

In efforts to intentionally create an environment of self-love, you're invited to implore these 8 steps.

1. Acknowledge and grow awareness of self-doubt or insecurities you may have.

    ▪ Allow yourself to make mistakes.

2. Forgive yourself for being so critical of you.

   - We've spoken about self-criticism. One notion that you will have to implement is to stop comparing yourself to others. Shift from being your biggest bully to engaging in being your biggest supporter.

3. Allow yourself to be curious about you and your needs.

   - Instead of just functioning, tap into your desires and needs. What would happen if you didn't wait for someone else to give these things to you and instead you explored ways of how you can provide these things to yourself.

4. Connect with yourself.

   - Identify what's important for you to feel love. Whatever your response is, start providing these acts to yourself.

5. Process doubts and fears that may arise.

   - These things are here for a reason. When you ignore it, that's just suppressing what's coming up. Processing is "the work" that's required to move through the doubts and fears so you can move closer to self-love and compassion.

6. Become your biggest cheerleader.

   - You are worthy of the cheer and praise. Sometimes you have to root for yourself.

7. Exercising an Attitude of Gratitude

   - Everything is energy and expressing gratitude is energetic. When you choose to live a life in a state of gratitude, you apply intentionality to pause and take note of what is working well in your life. As you begin to pay particular attention to your experience, you enhance the power to change the trajectory of your life and truly move through your healing journey.

8. Trust yourself to make good decisions for yourself.

Take each step one by one as you move towards letting love flow on you and through you.

When we talk about self-love, we are talking about gentleness, loving, kindness, and understanding. The same understanding that you would provide to a friend who is going through a hard time. Loving yourself means showing yourself that same form of gentleness that you would give someone else.

When we talk about being intentional in connecting to your most favorite self through love, the practice of gentleness would be in your best interest. Exploring ways to heal and support yourself is the foundation of loving yourself on purpose.

At any given time, you can give yourself what you need. With understanding that there is not an age limit or requirement necessary for you to shower yourself with love. In the forward of this book, Terry Gadson, PhD talked about self-love and self-care not being a luxury but being your divine access. You're not only deserving of loving yourself but it's also your right to know what loving yourself means to you. How are you pouring into you? The answer to this is vital. Treating yourself well and being able to show up in your authenticity is directly correlated to how you love yourself.

As you move through your journey, I welcome you to honor the progress that you do make along the way. It will not always be easy and some days you will feel defeated. On the days that all you did was breathe, know that's enough. Not every day is going to be a day where you feel you conquered the world. Guess what? That means you are human. This is where it will be important to ensure you exercise implementation of self-compassion.

Overall, promoting and exploring self-love is all about making small modifications in your life. Are you committed to loving yourself a little more than you did yesterday? In what ways will you take action to be intentional about connecting with yourself?

May love be in Overflow. Flowing on You and Through you.

Affirmations:

i.   I respect my own boundaries and am only allowing people in my life that do the same.

ii.   I am making room to love all parts of me.

iii.   I am choosing to do my best and accepting that it's best.

Take this time to write down any reflections or notes about

Chapter 8: Let Love Flow on You and Through You.

What will loving yourself more look like?

_____

_____

_____

_____

_____

_____

_____

_____

_____

_____

_____

_____

_____

_____

_____

_____

_____

_____

"It's time to be more of who you are and less of what they want you to be."

- Samiyrah Bennett

Authentically You

Stay True to You: Authentically You

Who are you? Do you even know?

Seriously, think about how you would answer.

Outside of your roles, material things, responsibility, and occupation, who are you? The answer you provide to this question is directly linked to your authentic self. Truth occurs when you are consciously connected to your core values and living a life that mirrors who and what you truly feel like you are inside. The process of being connected to your core values is what makes room for your authenticity to bloom.

As I begin writing this chapter, it is allowing me to reflect and recall a time when I really struggled with showing up as my authentic self and defining what that meant for me. From 5th grade to high school, I received my education from an institution that was predominantly filled with Caucasian students. 1 of about 10 African American females in the entire upper school at the time, I found myself desperately wanting to "fit in" but sometimes unsure of how. Code switching was at an all-time high and if we're being honest, truly compromising my authenticity. For those who may be reading this and not sure what 'code switching' means, it can be defined as altering your behavior, speech and/or expression in efforts to bring comfort to others while trying to be 'seen' by others or receive equal treatment. It can also be understood as the 'adaptive self.' The adaptive self prioritizes being liked, fitting in and looking to get along with others even if at the risk of abandoning true self. The experience of trying to connect with others while abandoning my core was jeopardizing me living in my truth. As it became more apparent, I began to give myself permission to show up how I wanted to. How I needed to. Come junior/senior year, I was accepting of how I was, why I was and who I was, with determination to stay loyal to my true values. This energy would carry me through my college years.

However, once entering the 'workforce', I found my true self fading into the background again. That feeling of needing to be someone or something else in order for others to connect with me was creeping back up. All because in my earlier years, I had been programmed by society and taught to believe that what, who and how I truly felt were inappropriate and unacceptable. Although that same feeling of drifting from my authenticity was creeping up, there was a difference. This time, I realized I was boxing myself in again but a lot sooner than my high school years. I guess maturity and life experience had some assistance with this. It's been a while now since I made the commitment to show up just as I am with the understanding that those that are for me will connect and what/who I am for, will not miss me.

If I could share 3 laws to live by with myself at "senior year" and in the beginning of my career in the 'workforce', it would be:

1. Be curious of who you are.
2. Be Bold in your presentation.
3. Take up Space unapologetically.

May you be encouraged to welcome these laws into your experience. As you, the reader, travel on your journey of life, I invite you to bring these statements with you as well. You are deserving of being firm in who you are, bold in your presentation and to unapologetically take up the space that you require. One thing I know for certain, it is never too late to connect with your core values and commit to showing up more authentically.

In order to be true to you, there must be an addressing of the parts of you that you've abandoned. Stop waiting for other people to give you permission on what you need to do in your life.

With authenticity comes vulnerability. You will be required to be vulnerable enough to explore the ways that you've abandoned your true self. Admitting to the ways that you have shown up in unauthentic ways is one of the foundational steps of radical authenticity. Facing the truth of self-deception is the humbling first step on any genuine journey of self-understanding and self-liberation (Bradford, 2019).

Standing firm in your authenticity also requires acceptance of a true self without needing any kind of validation or assurance from outside stimulus. As you begin to connect more and more to your true values, it will be imperative for you to release self-judgment or worry about the judgment that may come from others. Truly doing what is in your best interest without seeking validation from other people. This breeds confidence. Remaining consciously connected to your core values and mirroring what that means for you helps to boost self-esteem. The kind of self-esteem that allows you to walk into the room without wondering what everyone else is thinking about your presentation, outfit, behavior and/or expression.

Take note of how you may be trying to fit in or modify yourself in hopes that others will feel more comfortable in your presence.

Repeat after me: *"I'm not compromising self for the pleasure of others."*

Now is a good time to make yourself a promise moving forward. The promise may be to stand in who you truly are, what you represent, what you feel, what you like/don't like and/or consciously choosing to adhere to your core values. What would your life look like if you made room to present your true you? Staying committed to these actions is what leads you to being truly authentic.

One of my favorite tag lines is 'authenticity reigns supreme.' Authenticity reigns supreme means that nothing will get you further in life than being yourself and standing in all that that means for you.

I've come to realize that many of us are looking to be accepted and/or validated by other people. And it's not necessarily our fault. Most of those feelings come from how we were raised and interpersonal experiences we've had over the years. Along the way, you may have literally been subconsciously taught to seek external validation before validating yourself. (For example: As a child finishes dressing themselves and then asking a parental figure, "Do I look pretty?" If you consistently do this, it is programmed that you look to other people to define how you feel about yourself. An approach that I find helpful in breaking this cycle with my daughter is asking her how she feels she looks and then building from there.) When it comes time to be authentically you, you'll have to do the work of accepting, validating and affirming yourself without needing to receive these things from other people first.

I challenge you to search, find and connect with yourself. Then choose to be just that. Just as you are.

This process of connecting with authenticity can also be referred to as self-actualization. Psychologist, Abraham Maslow is well known for his work in identifying a human hierarchy of needs. In this hierarchy pyramid he describes tiers of the needs which include safety, basic needs, esteem and relationships. At the top of this hierarchy is the notion of self-actualization. This encompasses the ability to recognize your full potential and who you are.

It is through understanding your full potential that leads you to your authentic self.

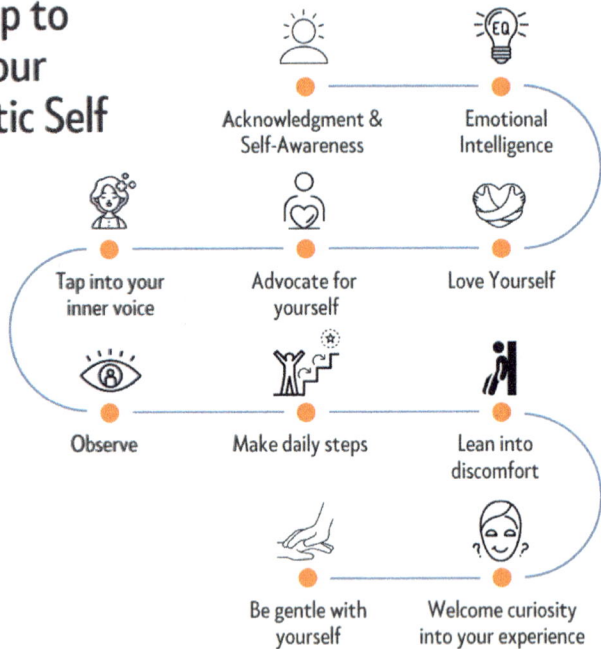

Roadmap to Being Your Authentic Self

- *Acknowledgment & Self Awareness* (It's time to fully step into who you are at your core. Bring attention to what you're feeling and acknowledge if you're ready to do something different.)
- *Emotional Intelligence* (With empathy, manage the feelings you may be experiencing.)
- *Tap into your inner voice* (Get clear on what is coming up for you.)
- *Advocate for yourself* (Stand firm in your values while honoring your worth.)

- *Love Yourself* (Continue to let love flow on you and through you as you move through the journey of connecting within.)

- *Observe* (Practice the pause between stimulus and response - Is this what I truly want to do, to say, to be.)

- *Make daily steps* (Every day is a new day, and you get to choose to show up just as you are.)

- *Lean into discomfort* (Surrender to what will bring you closer to showing up as your truest self.)

- *Welcome curiosity into your experience* (Allowing you to notice & explore the ways you show up.)

- *Be gentle with yourself* (Understanding the more you practice the more it will become automatic to be you without judgment or self-criticism.)

The greatest journey that you will ever embark on is the journey towards your most favorite self. Your favorite version of self is defined as the you that you feel most connected with, the you that experiences the most inner peace and joy.

If you feel that you remain looking for validation or approval, I encourage you to ask yourself why? Why do I need someone else to say 'yes' to me before I say 'yes' to myself? Who or where did you learn that from? After you answer those questions, move forward and challenge it.

Be open, be curious and fall in love with the real you. And guess what? You get to drown out the external noise and truly determine what that means for you.

I want you to make a commitment to stay connected and true to you. When the fear of what others may think arises, acknowledge the experience of fear, and then intentionally choose to show up as you are unapologetically. Deal?

You're invited to remember that you're in that room for a reason, in that community for a reason and sitting at that table for a reason. You're involved in that network for a reason. The reason is because you belong. Simply belonging because you are you. May you connect in ways that provide ease for you to stand in this truth. You belong because you are you without needing to modify for others to recognize.

The time is now. The time to be more of who you are and less of what they want you to be. Let's Go!

Affirmations:

i.   I don't have to be anyone but myself.

ii.   I am exploring ways to trust myself.

iii. Who I am is more than enough.

iv.   I belong because I am who I am.

Take this time to write down any reflections or notes about

Chapter 9: Stay True To You.

Speak to your inner self. What are you proud of?

How will you commit to letting your true self shine more?

_____

_____

_____

_____

_____

_____

_____

_____

_____

_____

_____

_____

_____

_____

_____

"When you find yourself in a cycle of habits that are breaking your spirit, feeling forced, and that you're being steered further away from your ideal self, these are general clues that you are in a toxic cycle."

- Samiyrah Bennett

Break The Cycle

"You have the power to say: This is not how my story will end."
- Christine Mason Miller

Now that we have navigated the foundational methods of how you can connect to your most favorite self, you may find yourself at a crossroads. One side of the road is the 'you' that has been doing what you've been doing. You know, the same ol' thang but expecting different results. Then, on the other side is your most favorite version waiting for you with open arms. The latter version of you is waiting for you to do the work it takes to get to the other side of the road. The most beautiful thing about being at a crossroad is that you are in control of making the decision whether you're going to go to the left or are you going to go to the right. Yes, it comes down to you making a decision. Making a choice to do something different. If you entertain the same patterns, you'll find yourself in the same cycle.

In the human experience it is common to find yourself in cycles. Cycles can be healthy or destructive in nature. Sometimes these cycles can be found in the everyday task. For example, deciding to watch the same movie over and over during distressing times because it brings comfort, predictability, and joy. Cycles can also be more problematic such as, repeatedly dating the "same kind of partner" but just in different bodies. Hmmm, you can relate, huh? Me too. So, let's keep reading.

Cycles become problematic when you constantly find yourself engaged in those patterns that are harmful, toxic, and/or unhealthy. You may find yourself repeating the same behavior that leads to distressing circumstances. Even if you recognize the behavior to be unhealthy or toxic, the behavior is repeated because you find it familiar. Humans like what is familiar and even if it is subconscious, there's a high probability that although a behavior causes distress, a human will re-engage (Levy,

2000). This notion is known as repetition compulsion. In psychoanalytic theory, psychoanalysis, Sigmund Freud, coined the notion "humans have compulsions to repeat" with suggestion of the behaviors that are repeated most are painful situations and feelings (Levy, 2000). This became known as repetitive compulsion.

Typically, these patterns are deep rooted from childhood. The patterns mirror things you witnessed, were taught, what you learned about relationships through modeled behavior, etc. These are most likely coping mechanisms that you are inclined to repeat as an adult including those experiences that were not so good for you. Your mind and body literally create and crave the hurtful cycles because it's designed to pull towards the recognizable.

When behaviors are compulsively repeated, there's a subconscious desire to want to break the cycle and make the situation "right" this time around. Ultimately, it is an impulse to gain control of the circumstance(s). So often, during the cycle, you don't realize you are partaking in the same behavior until it happens. You may then find yourself saying things like, "I keep meeting the same guy," "This just keeps happening," "I always end up in _____[this]_____ situation." Again, when you are ready for change, you have the power to decide to entertain alternative behavior.

What remains true, is that the human brain develops programming that shapes behavior. As we discussed in the first chapter about the concept of neuroplasticity, there is an awareness that although we have been conditioned to show up in what is familiar, we also have the ability to create new experiences. The shift to breaking the cycle is conducted by approaching toxic patterns with new thoughts, beliefs, and actions.

It's time to stop engaging in behaviors that only connect you to pain, suffering, and destructive paths. You are allowed to take an alternative route. It will have to start with you giving yourself permission to grow an awareness and the desire to want to do something about it.

The notion of compulsively repeating behaviors even when they are not in our best interest is truly complexed. However, it is possible to disengage and formulate new, healthier cycles.

After you've acknowledged the cycle and decided to do something about it, here are 7 approaches you can take to address your subconscious actions:

1. Commit to staying curious about the patterns that are causing harm in your life.

2. Process and explore the patterns with a licensed therapist or counselor.

3. Do the work to address deep rooted insecurities.

4. Decide to engage in specific therapies like Cognitive Behavioral Therapy (CBT), Dialectical Behavior Therapy (DBT) or Eye Movement Desensitization and Reprocessing (EMDR) to assist the brain in forming new, positive cognitions (ways of thinking).

5. Develop healthy coping mechanisms that allow you to live a more intentional life.

6. Learn to provide yourself with self-affirming thoughts to remind yourself when you're choosing healthy patterns in your best interest.

7.   Gift yourself with compassion and grace. Undoing years of
      conditioning is hard work. Be easy on yourself.

I want you to take inventory and evaluate your current circumstance(s).
What pattern do you find yourself in over and over again? It may be a
toxic pattern involved with a romantic relationship, a friendship, family
member, work situation or it may be the relationship with self. As you
have moved through the literature of this book, I wonder what cycles
have been coming up for you that may be time to break. As it was stated
earlier, the most important relationship is the relationship with yourself.
So, I ask, why are you staying committed to a cycle and pattern that
continuously breaks you down?

Most times when people think of breaking cycles, they automatically start
thinking about the relationships they have with other people in their lives.
While you can most definitely be involved in cycles that are toxic in
nature with other people, you can also be in unhealthy patterns with
yourself. Harmful patterns with yourself appear in ways of limited beliefs,
self-destruction/sabotage, doubting yourself more than you believe in
yourself, hanging out with people that do not match where you want to
go in your life, falling into a pattern of shame and finding yourself
focusing on your challenges rather than your strengths. Does any of this
sound familiar? Generally, you may repeat the behavior subconsciously
(without awareness) and this is simply because it is familiar to you. No
matter how uncomfortable that said behavior or thought is, you may
continue to repeat it in attempts to attain a different outcome.

You're doing the same thing and expecting different results.
Unfortunately, taking this approach may be what keeps you stagnant and
postponing the opportunity to connect with your greatest capabilities.

What if you choose to do more of the unfamiliar in efforts to break toxic cycles?

It is human nature to seek comfort; so, it makes sense that you will automatically choose to consistently go back to what feels familiar. However, familiarity does not equate to healthy.

Until you commit to changing unhealthy patterns that continue to present themselves in your experience, you will remain in the cycle that is stunting your growth. Don't you want to thrive? If so, you will be required to get rid of old habits and do something different than you have always done. Breaking the cycle is what leads you to a life of living on purpose. You're no longer going with the flow; you are being intentional about taking the tangible steps it takes to truly connect with the most favorite version of you. The version you were interested in when you first started reading this book. Are you going to leave them hanging now or will you be willing to explore the next steps to put what you learned into practice? I hope it's the latter. I truly hope you find a way to choose your wellness with confidence and conviction.

With a conscious choice, the cycle can begin shifting with a decision that you will be intentional about taking the steps needed to evolve towards the most favorite version of you. The version you find yourself learning to fall in love with over and over.

Repetitive behaviors provide humans a way to cope (negatively and positively) while navigating through life's journey. These coping skills can be healthy and support your overall wellbeing while others are simply destructive. When you find yourself in a cycle of habits that are breaking your spirit, feeling forced and that you're being steered further away from your ideal self, these are general clues that you are in a toxic cycle. As you attain more awareness of what is detrimental to your overall wellness, may you find yourself connected to healing tools that disrupt the negative patterns.

Truth be told, the cycle you're too uncomfortable letting go of is what is keeping you in the discomfort of feeling "stuck" and "broken". Have you heard of the phrase, "You have to do something different in order to get something different?" This concept implies that if you are eager to see your life or experience of a situation change, it will require you to be transparent about where you are and where you want to be. So, if you are feeling like you are not moving or what you want is not coming to you, I encourage you to assess the situation and recognize patterns that may be keeping you stagnant.

Along the journey of breaking a toxic cycle, you will notice that you will often need to come back to self. This includes mirror work, which means taking an honest look at yourself and accepting all of you. Mirror work provides an opportunity to see not just the surface of what you present but the beauty and all the layers that are encompassed within you. It really is meeting yourself with complete honesty of where you are, where you want to go and the steps you need to take to meet your true needs. As you begin to start practicing seeing your whole self, it will be important to be gentle with yourself while displaying love and self-affirming vibes. Coming back to self also includes inner child work. You'll have to be able to get curious about needs that were not met as a child and are screaming for attention as your adult self. Each time you come back to yourself, it will be important to bring effort, respect, empathy, love, kindness, and compassion.

In this moment right now, you have the power to decide whether you're going to continuously do the things that you have always done or are you going to take the information you learned and apply it into your life. Remember, you don't have to take all the steps at one time, but you can take inventory of the *next* step towards your best interest.

Earlier we discussed the patterns you may find yourself in even when you know that it goes against your authenticity. At this moment, you get to decide if that unproductive cycle will end with you. You have the power to break the cycle and live a more intentional life. It will require you to tap into places you have been avoiding for so long.

Being in the Mental Health profession for almost 20 years, I have witnessed many people on their healing and wellness journeys. What I've observed with most adults who have decided to prioritize their wellness, is that they've also made the choice to break a cycle that continuously shows up.

Just know that when you do decide to intentionally start breaking the cycle, there will be some things that get in your way that will seem challenging. In these moments, I want you to remember why you have decided to start changing the narrative. Some things that will arise as you try to move forward will be things like self-doubt, inner critic, child issues, fear, and all sort of things from your past. Understand that when these experiences come to pass, you'll have opportunity to explore them AND not allow them to keep you sitting still. It will be helpful to accept them for what they are and then consciously choose to continue to move towards your breakthrough as you break the cycle of doing the things that you've always done. Deal?

3 ways that you can start being a cycle breaker:

1. Be honest with what you're participating in and how it is actually working against you.
2. Admit that you are deserving of much better than what you've been giving yourself.
3. Choose to unplug from anything that doesn't align with your most favorite self.

Add 2 more ways that you will intentionally implement being a cycle breaker, starting today:

4. _____

_____

_____

5. _____

_____

_____

It's now on you to be the person you have always wanted to be. To start intentionally engaging in action steps that will bring you closest to your most favorite version of you. Mind your Business so you can live well and Take Good Care of Yourself. It's time to break the cycle!

You've now completed reading through the foundational steps to help you live more intently. May you be encouraged to utilize the strategies in your daily life in efforts to pour into yourself. As you continue along your healing journey, use this book as a blueprint to live well. Your favorite version is waiting for you. Take the knowledge and apply it so you can intentionally mind the business of YOU.

Affirmations:

i.   I am committed to doing what's in the best interest of me.

ii. The cycle of not addressing my personal needs ends with me.

iii. I am deserving of creating a supportive self-narrative.

Take this time to write down any reflections or notes about

Chapter 10: Break the Cycle.

Breaking the cycle takes commitment.

What cycle do you need to break?

What tangible actions can you take to break the cycle and form new,

improved, and healthy patterns for you?

_____

_____

_____

_____

_____

_____

_____

_____

_____

_____

_____

_____

_____

POST-ASSESSMENT

This assessment should be used to monitor your progress towards shifting the narrative.

Instructions: Circle "Y" for **Yes** and "N" for **No** for each question asked.

I have an enhanced understanding of the foundational steps I need to take in order to walk towards my most favorite self.

Y   N

I'm now committed to connecting with people and experiences that bring me peace and joy.

Y   N

I've learned alternative practices that I can begin using so I don't feel "stuck."

Y   N

I am looking forward to remaining curious in exploring ways that connect me with my authentic self.

Y   N

I've been provided with strategies and resources to help me start getting out of my head and into my life.

Y   N

If you answered "Y" to 3 or more of these statements, you are well on your way to enhancing your well-being. Your most favorite self is waiting for you to show up so keep making steps towards doing your best in all systems of your life. May you have continued favor as you work on developing self, connecting to spirituality, and transforming your wellness.

ABOUT THE AUTHOR

Samiyrah Bennett is a clinical social worker and licensed clinical psychotherapist in the states of New York and New Jersey. With almost 20 years' experience in the mental health field, Samiyrah serves as a mental health clinician, advocate, educator, and speaker. As a well-informed provider, Samiyrah provides useful strategies to assist her clients decrease anxiety, self-doubt and self-defeating thoughts while increasing a sense of empowerment, self-confidence, and execution of goals.

She's a change agent that is dedicated to honor and enrich the lives of individuals who chose to live life intentionally.

Samiyrah's mission is accomplished through individual, couple, and group work. Providing safe spaces for each of her clients. She is determined to help people tap into their inner selves and learn coping skills that allow them to live on purpose while promoting mental health and wellness.

Samiyrah has a well-constructed counseling business that is flexible when it comes to catering to clients' needs and services. Being able to provide clients with consistency, predictability and supportive services are all things that Samiyrah prioritizes.
Whether virtual or in person, when it comes to making impact, Samiyrah has a unique and dynamic way of providing psychoeducation, coping skills and encouragement all while being relatable. A sought-after speaker,

Samiyrah has been invited to speak for local organizations such as, the New York State Senator office, podcasts, and local hospitals. She also provides wellness workshops for various businesses and companies. As an award-winning community worker, Samiyrah has been recognized by the Westchester Department of Community Mental Health for outstanding services as a Westchester County Network Affiliate.

Samiyrah is clinically trained, and trauma informed. The evidence-based practices that she utilizes include cognitive behavioral therapy, mindfulness and EMDR (Eye movement, desensitization, and reprocessing). Through intentional living strategies and navigating mental wellness, Samiyrah not only shows up for her clients but she teaches them practical skills so they can show up for themselves.

Learn more and stay in community with her by visiting her website at www.SamiyrahBennettLCSW.org.

Additional Resources

The resources below are only for you if you're open to gaining additional tools to help you with the next steps in your healing journey.

Check out the 'The On Purpose Shop' section over at www.SamiyrahBennettLCSW.com for eBooks, merchandise, free downloads and more.

CONGRATULATIONS!

You've completed navigating the 10 foundational steps to take in order to connect with your most favorite self. I am so proud of the way you have chosen to commit to doing the work. Remember, doing the work includes taking action. May you receive love, light, ease, and peace on the next steps you will make to continue on your healing journey. And through it all, may you be determined to intentionally mind the business of you. Take Good Care of Yourself.

In wellness,

Samiyrah Bennett, MSW, LCSW

RESOURCES FOR THERAPY

The following list can be used if you're ready to take the next step on your healing journey and connect with a therapist. Feel free to pass the following contact information to a friend or family member who may be interested in connecting with a therapist.

- www.therapyforblackgirls.com
- www.therapyforblackmen.org
- www.psychologytoday.com
- www.openpathcollective.org
- www.therapyforlatinx.com
- www.blackfemaletherapists.com
- www.blackmaletherapists.com
- www.cliniciansofcolor.org

Choosing therapy is choosing life well and on purpose.

HELPFUL HOTLINES

SAMHSA (Substance Abuse and Mental Health Services Administration): 800.662.HELP (4357)

SAMHSA (Substance Abuse and Mental Health Services Administration) – Disaster Distress Helpline: 800.985.5990 or Text "TalkWithUs" to 66746

National Suicide Prevention Helpline: 800.273.TALK (8255)

National Domestic Violence Hotline: 800.799.7233 or text "LOVEIS" to 22522

National Alliance on Mental Illness (NAMI) Helpline: 800.950.NAMI (6264)

National Eating Disorders Association (NEDA) Helpline:
800.931.2237
Rape Abuse and Incest National Network (RAINN):
800.656.4673

The Trevor Project (LGTBQ):
866.488.7386 or Text "START" to 678678

Instagram:

@SamiyrahBennettLCSW

Email:

Samiyrah@SamiyrahBennettLCSW.org

Website:

www.SamiyrahBennettLCSW.org

REFERENCES

Beauchamp, T. L., & Childress, J. F. (2001). *Principles of biomedical ethics (5th ed.).* New York: Oxford University Press. https://www.apa.org/gradpsych/2014/04/corner.

Bradford, Ken. "Radical Authenticity." *Existential Analysis*, vol. 30, no. 1, Jan. 2019, pp. 117+. *Gale Academic OneFile*, link.gale.com/apps/doc/A575197091/AONE?u=nysl_se_hkdpl&sid=bookmark-AONE&xid=946400df.

Cascio, C. N., O'Donnell, M. B., Tinney, F. J., Lieberman, M. D., Taylor, S. E., Strecher, V. J., & Falk, E. B. (2016). Self-affirmation activates brain systems associated with self-related processing and reward and is reinforced by future orientation. *Social cognitive and affective neuroscience*, 11(4), 621–629.

Daugherty, T. K., Julian, H. M., Lynch, N. M., Chen, S. J., Whipple, T. L., & Ginsburg, A. F. (2016). *Beyond the absence of disease or infirmity: the case for sexual wellness.* College Student Journal, 50(3), 404+. https://link.gale.com/apps/doc/A466783189/AONE?u=nysl_se_hkdpl&sid=bookmark-AONE&xid=bd646c9b.

Hill, Lauryn. "Do Wop (That Thing)." The Miseducation of Lauryn Hill, Marley Music, Inc, 1998, track 5. Genius, https://genius.com/Lauryn-hill-doo-wop-that-thing-lyrics.

KH;, Kays JL;Hurley RA;Taber. "The Dynamic Brain: Neuroplasticity and Mental Health." *The Journal of Neuropsychiatry and Clinical Neurosciences*, U.S. National Library of Medicine, https://pubmed.ncbi.nlm.nih.gov/22772660/.

Lally, Phillipps, et al. "How are habits formed: Modelling habit formation in the real world." *European Journal of Social Psychology Eur. J. Soc. Psychol.* 40, 998 - 1009 (2010) Published online 16 July 2009 in Wiley Online Library (wileyonlinelibrsry.com).

Levy, Michael (2000) *A Conceptualization of the Repetition Compulsion, Psychiatry*, 63:1, 45-53, DOI: 10.1080/00332747.2000.11024893.

Merriam-Webster. (n.d.). Affirm. In Merriam-Webster.com dictionary. Retrieved January 15, 2022, from https://www.merriam-webster.com/dictionary/affirm.

Merriam-Webster. (n.d.). Self-love. In Merriam-Webster.com dictionary. Retrieved January 27, 2022, from https://www.merriam-webster.com/dictionary/self-love.

Quan, P., Wang, W., Chu, C, & Hou, L. (2018). Seven days of mindfulness-based cognitive therapy improves attention and coping style. *Social Behavior and Personality,* 46(3), 421-430. 430. https://doi.org/10.2224/sbp.6623.

Rosa, Andreia Martins, et al. "Plasticity in the human visual cortex: an ophthalmology-based perspective." *BioMed Research International*, annual 2013. *Gale Academic OneFile*,

link.gale.com/apps/doc/A373373067/AONE?u=nysl_se_hkdpl&sid=bookmar
k-AONE&xid=07bc3995. Accessed 4 Nov. 2021.

SAMHSA (2015). *The Eight Dimensions of Wellness*. Author. Retrieved from
http://www.samhsa.gov/wellness-initiativeeight-dimensions-wellness.

Made in the USA
Coppell, TX
23 June 2022